Acts of the Apostles

in Ten Minutes a Day

Mason Barge

TABLE OF CONTENTS

Introduction

I have gotten the most benefit from reading the Bible when I sit down and really concentrate on thoroughly understanding what I am reading. That is, when I go slow and do not try to read more than I can realistically absorb at one sitting. And almost always, it is helpful to listen to some basic extra information about it.

Thus, I have structured this book to present *The Acts of the Apostles* in the format I find most helpful: Manageable bites, stopping to chew when my mouth is full.

You might want to read more than one lesson a day: your choice. But pace yourself so that you can fully absorb the material. This isn't a race. You don't have anything to prove. Enjoy it! The "Gospel of the Holy Spirit" (as *Acts* is sometimes called) will bring you even closer to God and His Son.

In just a few weeks, you are really going to understand how the early church came into existence, how the Holy Spirit came to dwell among us after Christ ascended to Heaven, and especially, how the Apostle Paul spread Christianity to the Gentiles: first to the Greek towns of Turkey, then throughout the Roman Empire, and thus, ultimately, to us.

The book is presented without external ("systematic") theology, so it should be acceptable to any Christian — Catholic, Protestant, Orthodox, or any other Christian denomination. There are not a lot of contentious theological issues in *Acts*, but if there is a matter of disagreement, my practice is to try to present all sides and let the reader choose between them.

Understand, however, that the scholarship herein is Christian. The underlying assumption throughout is that the Bible is the inspired and inerrant word of God.

(*Note*: To avoid confusion, the "w" in "word of God" will not be capitalized herein, unless it refers to the person of Christ – i.e. "In the beginning was the Word.")

The impetus for this series is the online daily devotionals provided by Daily Prayer, a free service of Daily Prayer Ministries, Inc. This is a non-profit non-denominational ministry, available every day online.

I have spent a lot of time researching the accuracy and readability of Bible translations — including translating many books of the New Testament myself! The primary translation in this volume is the *Berean Standard Bible*, a fairly literal translation. We will sample several others, however; just rest assured that I have double-checked them for accuracy and freedom from theological distortion or other bias.

Acts 1 – The Ascension

Day 1 - Prologue

Acts 1:1-3

In my first book, O Theophilus, I wrote about all that Jesus began to do and to teach, until the day He was taken up to heaven, after giving instructions through the Holy Spirit to the apostles He had chosen. After His suffering, He presented Himself to them with many convincing proofs that He was alive. He appeared to them over a span of forty days and spoke about the kingdom of God.

Commentary

Acts tells the story of the Apostolic Age of the early Christian church, with particular emphasis on the arrival of the Holy Spirit, the ministry of the apostles, and especially the ministry of Paul of Tarsus (which takes up two-thirds of the book). The early chapters, set in Jerusalem, discuss Jesus' Resurrection and Great Commission, His Ascension (including His promise to return), the start of the Twelve Apostles' ministry, and the Day of Pentecost. The later chapters focus on Paul's conversion, his long journeys to spread Christianity to the Greek-speaking world, the many churches he founded, and finally, his arrest and imprisonment in Rome.

The entire book was written by a man named Luke, who also wrote the *Gospel of Luke*. Luke was a physician and a very early disciple of Christ. He was not one of the apostles, however; and the prologue to his gospel (Luke 1:1-4) strongly implies that he was not an eyewitness to the events of Christ's life. He wrote some parts of *Acts* as he wrote his gospel: from information given to him by others. Some other parts, however, unlike his gospel, are written in the first person and thus appear to be written from first-hand knowledge.

Certainly he knew Paul well. Paul names him in three epistles: "Luke, the dearly loved physician" (Colossians 4:14), "Mark . . . and Luke, my fellow workers" (Philemon 1:24), and "Only Luke is with me" (2 Timothy 4:11).

Acts of the Apostles was written in refined biblical (*koine*) Greek, and the tone and style are consistent from the first verse to the last. From this and several other clues, scholars have concluded that Luke was an educated man and most likely (and rather remarkably) a Gentile.

Nobody really knows who "Theophilus" was. There are a lot of theories about his identity. Very likely, though, this is not an actual name. The word *theophilus* is a Greek compound noun meaning "friend of God" — thus, the book is addressed to every friend of God, meaning whomever is reading it in faith. In other words, it is addressed to someone who will live over 2,000 years later: You!

Verses 1 to 3 reference the "first book" — *i.e.* the *Gospel of Luke* — and simply recap the events after the crucifixion.

Background discussion: "Koine Greek"

(Editorial Note: This book will have "Discussions" from time to time, which do not apply directly to the Book of Acts. These might be interesting background facts, questions for discussion or contemplation, ideas for practical application in your life, etc. You can just skip these if you want to move along a bit faster.)

Prior to roughly 300 B.C., there were dozens of dialects of Ancient Greek. The New Testament was written in a dialect which evolved around 300 B.C. called "Koine Greek," *koine* being Greek for "common." This became the *lingua franca* of the Greek world (from about 300 B.C. to 500 A.D.) and was spoken from Spain to India! It was everybody's second language.

Its origin was the army of Alexander the Great, who conquered an empire from Greece to Egypt and India. He accumulated soldiers from every conquered tribe, and they needed to be able to communicate. There must have been 100 languages spoken in the Macedonian

Army. So, a simplified Greek dialect was standardized for Alexander's army and became the dialect of Greek spoken in trade throughout the Mediterranean world.

It was so pervasive that the first complete Jewish Bible (*Tanakh*) was compiled, not in Hebrew, but in Koine Greek (in Alexandria, completed in 132 B.C.).

Day 2 - The Ascension

Acts 1:4-11

And while they were gathered together, He commanded them: "Do not leave Jerusalem, but wait for the gift the Father promised, which you have heard Me discuss. For John baptized with water, but in a few days you will be baptized with the Holy Spirit."

So when they came together, they asked Him, "Lord, will You at this time restore the kingdom to Israel?"

Jesus replied, "It is not for you to know times or seasons that the Father has fixed by His own authority. But you will receive power when the Holy Spirit comes upon you, and you will be My witnesses in Jerusalem, and in all Judea and Samaria, and to the ends of the earth."

After He had said this, they watched as He was taken up, and a cloud hid Him from their sight. They were looking intently into the sky as He was going, when suddenly two men dressed in white stood beside them. "Men of Galilee," they said, "why do you stand here looking into the sky? This same Jesus, who has been taken from you into heaven, will come back in the same way you have seen Him go into heaven."

Commentary

The four Gospels do not give a detailed account of the Ascension. *Matthew* and *John* end with Jesus still on earth, while *Mark* and *Luke* describe his departure in a single sentence: "He was taken up into heaven and sat down at the right hand of God." (Mark 16:19; similarly, Luke 24:51.)

In writing the *Book of Acts*, Luke corrects the omission as the first order of business. If we have just finished reading *John*, and move on to the next book, we get a sense of continuity, because the first sentence of *Acts* picks up right where *John* left off!

The eleven remaining apostles, being devout Jews, have not given up the idea that Christ came to restore the Kingdom of Israel. This shows how ingrained the Mosaic Covenant was to the Jews; the Pharisees and Sadducees (ignoring the prophets!) taught that the Messiah would be a Jewish Messiah, not the savior of the Gentiles as well. But when the apostles ask if the day has arrived for the restoration of the kingdom of Israel, Christ gently rebukes and corrects them on two accounts. First, the timing is not for them to know; and second, their duty is to witness, not just to Israel, but "to the ends of the earth."

The "ends of the earth" has two meanings. The literal Greek translation is singular: "the end" of the earth, not "the ends." Thus, the passage indicates that Christ's word will live, and must continue to be spread, until the earth ceases to exist.

But the Greek text also can mean "the farthest point of the earth," so the English idiom "ends of the earth" is also a correct translation; Christ's word will be spread over the entire planet.

The passage ends with an account of the Ascension. The two men in white seem to be angels, but they might bring to mind the visions of Elijah and Moses, whom Matthew, Mark, and Luke all recount at the Transfiguration. (See, *e.g.*, Luke 9:28-36.)

Discussion Question

Jesus tells His followers, "In a few days you will be baptized with the Holy Spirit." How does this jibe with your concept of baptism? And who will be baptizing them?

This is an advanced issue of theology, presented for "discussion," not "decision"! And beware; denominations often have very fixed (and sometimes emotional) dogma on the subject of baptism.

4

Day 3 - The Death of Judas Iscariot

Acts 1:12-20

Then they returned to Jerusalem from the Mount of Olives, which is near the city, a Sabbath day's journey away. When they arrived, they went to the upper room where they were staying: Peter and John, James and Andrew, Philip and Thomas, Bartholomew and Matthew, James son of Alphaeus, Simon the Zealot, and Judas son of James. With one accord they all continued in prayer, along with the women and Mary the mother of Jesus, and with His brothers.

In those days Peter stood up among the brothers (a gathering of about a hundred and twenty) and said, "Brothers, the Scripture had to be fulfilled which the Holy Spirit foretold through the mouth of David concerning Judas, who became a guide for those who arrested Jesus. He was one of our number and shared in this ministry."

(Now with the reward for his wickedness Judas bought a field; there he fell headlong and burst open in the middle, and all his intestines spilled out. This became known to all who lived in Jerusalem, so they called that field in their own language Akeldama, that is, Field of Blood.)

> "For it is written in the book of Psalms:
> 'May his place be deserted;
> let there be no one to dwell in it,'
> and,
> 'May another take his position.'"

Commentary

Olivet is the same as the Mount of Olives, a pleasant place just outside Jerusalem. The phrase "a Sabbath day's journey" describes the distance a Jew was permitted (by the Pharisees) to walk on the Sabbath. Jews were basically forbidden from traveling on the Sabbath, but if necessary (to go to worship, for example) they could walk within a radius of 1000 yards from their residence.

We see the kernel of the Christian church in this passage; only 120 people, including 11 apostles and Jesus' family. It is the seed of a plant that will overgrow the entire earth, one day; but at this time, things seemed rather precarious. They were still hiding from the Jewish authorities, so they preferred a cramped upper room to the outdoors, which would have been a preferable place to meet for so many. Really, the rise of Christianity from such a small group is a miracle, when you think about the thousands of religious groups that have formed and then disappeared from history after their leader died.

Notice also that Peter is the first to speak. He has already become the leader, as was ordained by Christ. ("And I tell you that you are Peter, and on this rock I will build My church, and the gates of Hades will not prevail against it." Matthew 16:18)

The account of Judas' death in *Acts* seems to differ from the account in Matthew 27:3-10, which relates that Judas hanged himself. There is a third account of his death from a reliable source, an early Christian bishop named Papias, who wrote that Judas became swollen and had his gut burst by a chariot. The accounts can be reconciled, especially in the original Greek, but the big picture is more important than the details: Judas died a gruesome and lonely death, out of touch with his formerly beloved friends.

It would have been hard for them to know what happened to Judas. He had left without telling them where he was going, and being in seclusion, they were not in a position to investigate. None of them stayed in touch with him (which is why Peter has to tell everyone the account he has heard). They had to rely on rumor, and the rumors would have been scarce, since Judas was hardly a person of any importance in the city.

Day 4 - Matthias Chosen to Replace Judas

Acts 1:21-26

"Therefore it is necessary to choose one of the men who have accompanied us the whole time the Lord Jesus went in and out among us, beginning from John's baptism until the day Jesus was taken up from us. For one of these must become a witness with us of His resurrection."

So they proposed two men: Joseph called Barsabbas (also known as Justus) and Matthias. And they prayed, "Lord, You know everyone's heart. Show us which of these two You have chosen to take up this ministry and apostleship, which Judas abandoned to go to his rightful place."

Then they cast lots, and the lot fell to Matthias; so he was added to the eleven apostles.

Commentary

Judas was dead, and the little group thought it right to keep the number of apostles at twelve, as Jesus had done. Peter, who has assumed the mantle of leadership, decides on a single qualification, that the man be someone who had witnessed all the events of Jesus' life and resurrection, so that he might give first-hand witness to them.

Notice that in 1:20, Peter quotes Scripture that would authorize replacing Judas: "Let another take his office." (Psalm 109:8) This practice of requiring Biblical precedent is today sometimes called "Berean"; in fact, there is a Berean movement in modern Christianity, and we will see the source of the term in Acts 17. They strongly follow the practice of looking first to Scripture for specific guidance — a theological necessity often ignored today by clergy and parishioner alike, when they prefer to turn to their own opinions first (and sometimes solely!).

The procedure thereafter appears to have been one of consensus; Peter does not dictate. Two men emerged who seemed satisfactory to everyone; to decide between them, we today would probably put it to a vote. But they cast lots; in effect, they threw dice, trusting that God would intervene.

We might take a lesson from this. They avoided "church politics" as much as possible. And today, in fact, some Amish communities pull names out of a hat to decide which among them will become preachers! All the Amish are expected to know the Gospel; the men picked to lead worship and preach a sermon are not charismatic or popular leaders. They are servants. (*See* Matthew 23:8-12.)

Bonus Discussion: The Bereans

We will learn a bit more about the original Bereans in Chapter 17, but I wanted to take a second to thank the people of the modern Berean movement for all they have done for this book and for Christianity. All Scriptural citations, unless otherwise marked, come from the "Berean Standard Bible." If you want a trustworthy Bible, I give this translation a 10/10.

There is also a wonderful online Bible resource with a library of information called Bible Hub, which has some loose association with the BSB. (https://biblehub.com/) I have no connection to any of these organizations. My admiration is strictly arm's-length.

Acts 2 - Pentecost

Day 5 - The Coming of the Holy Spirit

Acts 2:1-13

When the day of Pentecost came, they were all together in one place. Suddenly a sound like a mighty rushing wind came from heaven and filled the whole house where they were sitting. They saw tongues like flames of fire that separated and came to rest on each of them. And they were all filled with the Holy Spirit and began to speak in other tongues as the Spirit enabled them.

Now there were dwelling in Jerusalem God-fearing Jews from every nation under heaven. And when this sound rang out, a crowd came together in bewilderment, because each one heard them speaking his own language.

Astounded and amazed, they asked, "Are not all these men who are speaking Galileans? How is it then that each of us hears them in his own native language? Parthians, Medes, and Elamites; residents of Mesopotamia, Judea and Cappadocia, Pontus and Asia, Phrygia and Pamphylia, Egypt and the parts of Libya near Cyrene; visitors from Rome, both Jews and converts to Judaism; Cretans and Arabs—we hear them declaring the wonders of God in our own tongues!"

Astounded and perplexed, they asked one another, "What does this mean?"

But others mocked them and said, "They are drunk on new wine!"

Commentary

Although most Bible translations refer to the sound made by the Holy Spirit as a "wind," the original Greek words also mean, literally, a "violent breath." And it would seem correct to view the wind, here, as the very breath of God. Remember that God breathed into Adam's nostril to give him life! (Genesis 2:7)

9

Christ had previously imparted the Spirit to the apostles by breathing on them (John 20:21-22). Thus, when the Holy Spirit is given more widely to Christ's followers, we might consider that it is the very breath of God, fulfilling Jesus' promise that He would not leave his followers alone, and perhaps bringing them life, or reassuring them of their eternal life.

Does "people speaking in many languages" sound familiar? It occurred in the Old Testament. In the story of the Tower of Babel (Genesis 11), God prevented men from building a tower "as high as heaven" by making them all speak different languages, and then He scattered them all over the earth.

But here, after Christ's Ascension, the Holy Spirit effectively does the opposite of what God did in the Tower of Babel. People have come to Jerusalem from all over the world. When the disciples speak, people from every nation can understand what is being said.

The gift of unity is one of Christ's gifts to those who will follow Him (although they often seem to reject the gift!). Knowledge of God had been given to the Hebrews in the Old Covenant; however, Christ had promised to spread his salvation not only to the Jews, but also to all people in the world. Where the Old Covenant divided humanity, the New Covenant brings them together.

Note that the Christians "began to speak in other tongues." The listeners did not begin to "hear" miraculously; rather, the disciples actually spoke in other languages.

Bonus discussion: "Pentecost"

We tend to think of Pentecost as a Christian holiday, the day when the Holy Spirit was given to us, but it was originally a Jewish holiday. The Hebrew name for it is *Shavuot*.

Do you remember when we said that the first complete Jewish Bible was written in Greek, around 300 B.C.? (Of course, the ancient scrolls from which this Bible were collected were written in Hebrew.) The Greek word Pentecost (pentēkostē), which means "fiftieth," was first used in this Bible as a reference to *Shavuot*, because *Shavuot* occurs 50 days after Passover.

There were three "pilgrimage festivals" in Judaism: Passover, *Shavuot*, and *Sukkot*. (*Sukkot* is sometimes called The Festival of Tabernacles, Tents, or Booths.) During these, all Israelites who were able were expected to make a pilgrimage to the Temple in Jerusalem, as commanded by the Torah.

Day 6 - Peter's Sermon at Pentecost (1)

Acts 2:14- 21

Then Peter stood up with the Eleven, lifted up his voice, and addressed the crowd: "Men of Judea and all who dwell in Jerusalem, let this be known to you, and listen carefully to my words. These men are not drunk, as you suppose. It is only the third hour of the day! No, this is what was spoken by the prophet Joel:

'In the last days, God says
I will pour out My Spirit on all people.
Your sons and daughters will prophesy,
your young men will see visions,
your old men will dream dreams.

Even on My menservants and maidservants
I will pour out My Spirit in those days,
and they will prophesy.
I will show wonders in the heavens above
and signs on the earth below,
blood and fire and billows of smoke.
The sun will be turned to darkness,
and the moon to blood,
before the coming of the great and glorious Day of the
Lord.
And everyone who calls on the name of the Lord
will be saved.'"

Commentary

At the end of the preceding verses, the followers of Christ were running around speaking different languages after the Holy Spirit descended upon them. Onlookers decided they were drunk. But Peter stands up to speak, and says, basically, "they aren't drunk; it's only 10 a.m."

At that time, Jews measured days and hours differently than we do. The Jewish day was about the same as ours — sunrise to sunset. Day ended precisely when three "stars" (two of them were actually planets) became visible.

But "hours" were very different. "Daytime hours" were a different length than "night hours," and they changed every day! No matter how long the daytime lasted, it had exactly 12 hours. In summer, when days are longer, Hebrew hours were correspondingly longer — perhaps 70 minutes. In the middle of winter, when days are short, an hour might have been only 50 minutes long. The third hour of the day would thus have started when the day was 1/6 over. So 10:00 a.m. is an approximation of the time of day.

Peter then launches into a long sermon, the first real sermon in Christian church history. He starts with one of the most convincing arguments that could be made to a Jewish crowd: that the events they were witnessing —the coming of the Holy Spirit—were prophesied in the Old Testament. Just like a good preacher today, he supports his sermon by citing Scripture.

His first such citation is a lengthy quote from *Joel*, in which Joel predicted a time when God would pour out his Spirit upon the earth. It doesn't exactly match what was happening, because these are not the "last days." But it is a foretaste. And the prophecy orients the listeners to the solemnity of the occasion. They are witnessing a momentous inflection point in the changing relationship of God and humanity.

This is the hand of God performing a major miracle; not some drunken silliness. God has come to earth in front of their very eyes!

Day 7 - Peter's Sermon (2)

Acts 2:22-31

"Men of Israel, listen to this message: Jesus of Nazareth was a man certified by God to you by miracles, wonders, and signs, which God did among you through Him, as you yourselves know. He was delivered up by God's set plan and foreknowledge, and you, by the hands of the lawless, put Him to death by nailing Him to the cross. But God raised Him from the dead, releasing Him from the agony of death, because it was impossible for Him to be held in its clutches.

David says about Him:

> 'I saw the Lord always before me;
> because He is at my right hand, I will not be shaken.
> Therefore my heart is glad and my tongue rejoices;
> my body also will dwell in hope,
> because You will not abandon my soul to Hades,
> nor will You let Your Holy One see decay.
> You have made known to me the paths of life;
> You will fill me with joy in Your presence.'

Brothers, I can tell you with confidence that the patriarch David died and was buried, and his tomb is with us to this day. But he was a prophet and knew that God had promised him on oath that He would place one of his descendants on his throne. Foreseeing this, David spoke about the resurrection of the Christ, that He was not abandoned to Hades, nor did His body see decay."

Commentary

Peter continues Christianity's first sermon, a proselytizing speech to a crowd that had gathered at the hubbub caused by the Holy Spirit's descent onto 120 followers of Christ. In the preceding verses, the first part of the speech, he quoted a lengthy prophecy from *Joel*, concerning miracles that would occur in the "last days."

In the first paragraph today, Peter ties Joel's prophecy of miracles to the life and resurrection of Jesus of Nazareth. He says that Jesus was "certified" to humanity by miracles; like a passport or identification, the miracles of Jesus served to identify him as the Messiah. The people whom He came to save were so wicked that they killed Him; but death could not hold Him.

In the next portion, Peter cites a psalm written by David, in which David prophesied that God "would not leave my soul in Hades." (Psalm 16:10) Peter ties this psalm to the fruit of the resurrection. He claims that David's prophecy predicted the time they had just witnessed. Jesus' resurrection was the fulfillment of an oath God had made to David.

The crowd already believed in the truth of David's prophecy. They were Jews and they had learned this in synagogue. Now Peter, in his role as the "rock upon which" Christ would found his church (Matthew 16:18), begins his work: to persuade the Jews that Christ had fulfilled David's prophecy.

Day 8 - Peter's Sermon (3)

Acts 2:32-39

God has raised this Jesus to life, to which we are all witnesses. Exalted, then, to the right hand of God, He has received from the Father the promised Holy Spirit and has poured out what you now see and hear. For David did not ascend into heaven, but he himself says:

> 'The Lord said to my Lord,
> "Sit at My right hand
> until I make Your enemies
> a footstool for Your feet."'

Therefore let all Israel know with certainty that God has made this Jesus, whom you crucified, both Lord and Christ!"

When the people heard this, they were cut to the heart and asked Peter and the other apostles, "Brothers, what shall we do?"

Peter replied, "Repent and be baptized, every one of you, in the name of Jesus Christ for the forgiveness of your sins, and you will receive the gift of the Holy Spirit. This promise belongs to you and your children and to all who are far off—to all whom the Lord our God will call to Himself."

Commentary

A large crowd has gathered — perplexed, perhaps excited, and possibly amused by the odd actions occurring around the building where the "upper room" was located. The people who had been blessed—Peter, the apostles, and approximately 110 other disciples—have gone out into the street. Having given the crowd a long introduction, with citation to the Old Testament, Peter here gets to the "nitty-gritty" of his message.

When they are told that they have crucified a man whom God had sent, the people in the crowd are horrified. They feel cut to the heart. Peter has convinced them that they have offended God, and they are ashamed and terrified. They beg Peter and the apostles to tell them what to do. Peter tells them to repent and to be baptized in Jesus' name; only in this way can they be cleansed of their sins, including specifically the sin of killing the Christ.

Peter has wasted no time in carrying out the mission Jesus left him. He is openly preaching that the crowd should become followers of a man who has recently been convicted of heresy and suffered execution for it. He is either going to create an evangelical backlash against the Jewish authorities for their murder of Jesus, or die trying.

If we remember back to the entirety of any of the Gospels, we see Peter finally becoming the man Jesus meant him to be. His actions are the consummation, the realization, of three years of painful training. He has been fully prepared and now, at the most opportune moment, he picks up the mantle of Christ — fully knowing it will cause his death — and puts it on his shoulders without hesitation. It is Peter who first dares to tell the world about the risen Christ.

Day 9 - The Enthusiasms of the Believers

Acts 2:40-47

With many other words he [Peter] testified, and he urged them, "Be saved from this corrupt generation." Those who embraced his message were baptized, and about three thousand were added to the believers that day.

They devoted themselves to the apostles' teaching and to the fellowship, to the breaking of bread and to prayer. A sense of awe came over everyone, and the apostles performed many wonders and signs.

All the believers were together and had everything in common. Selling their possessions and goods, they shared with anyone who was in need.

With one accord they continued to meet daily in the temple courts and to break bread from house to house, sharing their meals with gladness and sincerity of heart, praising God and enjoying the favor of all the people. And the Lord added to their number daily those who were being saved.

Commentary

Peter's sermon has been a huge success. He converted a large number of the Jews with his words and started the first church, the church in Jerusalem. The timeline and numbers are uncertain: The passage records that 3,000 were converted on the day of his sermon and that more were converted "daily," but it does not otherwise record numbers of people or amounts of time.

The first church is fervent, even fanatical. The members devote themselves to it, meeting every day to worship and forming a sort of commune, where property is shared freely. Not only do they meet to worship, but they also take their meals together.

Most remarkably, they meet in the temple courts, the public areas in front of the temple. Remember, only a few days earlier the apostles and a few followers had hidden themselves away, out of fear of the Jewish authorities. They were, rightfully, afraid for their lives. Now they are making a public spectacle of themselves. They are completely filled with the Holy Spirit, so much so that they concern themselves with almost nothing other than worship of God through Christ, even in the face of very real danger.

Discussion Question: Enthusiasm

The first Christians were filled with the Holy Spirit and lived in total enthusiasm for Christ. Look over the various lifestyle choices they made, such as sharing property and eating meals together, and compare them to how we live, today.

Should we model them more, perhaps by developing a more enthusiastic corporate experience on a daily basis? How and what might we do?

Acts 3 - Peter's Sermon

Day 10 - A Lame Man Healed

Acts 3:1-10

One afternoon Peter and John were going up to the temple at the hour of prayer, the ninth hour. And a man who was lame from birth was being carried to the temple gate called Beautiful, where he was put every day to beg from those entering the temple courts. When he saw Peter and John about to enter, he asked them for money.

Peter looked directly at him, as did John. "Look at us!" said Peter. So the man gave them his attention, expecting to receive something from them. But Peter said, "Silver or gold I do not have, but what I have I give you: In the name of Jesus Christ of Nazareth, get up and walk!"

Taking him by the right hand, Peter helped him up, and at once the man's feet and ankles were made strong. He sprang to his feet and began to walk. Then he went with them into the temple courts, walking and leaping and praising God.

When all the people saw him walking and praising God, they recognized him as the man who used to sit begging at the Beautiful Gate of the temple, and they were filled with wonder and amazement at what had happened to him.

Commentary

The Gospels, especially John's Gospel, show us that Christ's miracles had a specific purpose. They were not cheap tricks, nor did they represent a promise that God intended to relieve Jesus' followers of all disease and suffering. Rather, they were limited and specific signs that Christ had a special status, given by God. He performed only as many miracles as needed to announce His special status, the Messiah, the Son of God.

Because Christ has ascended at this point, one might expect that His power of working miracles, as signs that He was sent by God, would have gone with Him. Yet here we have Peter healing a lame man, much as Christ might have done.

We might suspect that Peter's miracles have a similar purpose: to announce and authenticate the divinity of the Holy Spirit. Most Christians believe that The Holy Spirit is God; and so, we might infer a strong similarity between the miracles of Christ and the miracles of the Holy Spirit performed though Peter.

(*Cf.* 1 Corinthians 1:20-25, where Paul teaches that the Jews will seek signs or miracles, but will "stumble" over the concept of Christ crucified; implying that they had already gotten all the signs and miracles they needed to point their way to salvation.)

Peter also tells the man to get up and walk "in the name of Jesus Christ of Nazareth." Remember, in John 11:43, Jesus simply used the words, "Lazarus, come out!" Thus, Peter is not pretending to heal by his own abilities, or even by dispensation from God the Father. His healing is a sign that, although Christ is gone, the Holy Spirit has come, just as Christ had promised. To ease the transition from Christ's physical presence on earth, Peter can heal by Christ's authority. In this sense, the miracles fulfill Jesus' promise that we would not be left along after His Ascension. (*See* John 14:15-25.)

It is fundamental to our faith as Christians that Christ did not leave us alone. In effect, He is still with us; for God dwells within us in the form of the Holy Spirit.

We might also see Peter's miracles as a transitional period, to cushion the shock of Christ's departure to those who had depended on his physical presence. Christ would not allow the church to die from the trauma of his departure. Perhaps the early church needed Christ-like signs from God to prove He was still with them. Perhaps our faith has become so lukewarm that we rarely enjoy the full power of the Holy Spirit.

In any case, like Christ's miracles, Peter's miracle is not a magic trick designed to lure in a few witnesses. It is, rather, a sign that God's person has remained active on earth even though Christ, Himself, has departed. Fittingly, this power is displayed through the apostle whom

Christ had named "the rock" upon which He would build His church. (Matthew 16:18)

Note that the Holy Spirit's presence is continuous and widespread. In early Judaism, God "resided" in the tabernacle or temple. There were also manifestations (called "theophanies"), such as the man who interacted with Abraham, or the burning bush. And Jesus, also, existed in a specific physical form. Today, however, God no longer lives in a specific spot on earth; rather, He resides in the heart of every Christian.

Day 11 - Peter Speaks in Solomon's Portico (1)

Acts 3:11-16

While the man clung to Peter and John, all the people were astonished and ran to them in the walkway called Solomon's Colonnade. And when Peter saw this, he addressed the people:

"Men of Israel, why are you surprised by this? Why do you stare at us as if by our own power or godliness we had made this man walk?

The God of Abraham, Isaac, and Jacob, the God of our fathers, has glorified His servant Jesus. You handed Him over and rejected Him before Pilate, even though he had decided to release Him. You rejected the Holy and Righteous One and asked that a murderer be released to you. You killed the Author of life, but God raised Him from the dead, and we are witnesses of the fact.

By faith in the name of Jesus, this man whom you see and know has been made strong. It is Jesus' name and the faith that comes through Him that has given him this complete healing in your presence."

Commentary

The man clinging to Peter and John is someone who has just been healed of lameness. The portico of Solomon was not really a portico (a covered walkway leading to a door) but a porch or colonnade on the east wall of the temple. It was a large and beautiful structure built of white stone. It measured roughly 350 yards in length; a lot of people could gather in it.

The meaning of the passage is straightforward. Peter continues to preach the gospel. Because Jesus' death occurred so recently, he emphasizes the crime that the Jewish authorities, and the people of Jerusalem themselves, have committed.

Peter is also, perhaps, concerned for the safety of himself and his brethren in Christ. Public opinion was mostly against Christ, as is obvious from the details of the Crucifixion; specifically, the crowd's demand that Barabbas be released rather than Jesus. It is in Peter's interest to see public opinion change, to temper the anti-Christ attitude in Jerusalem.

One wouldn't expect that he would soften the position of Caiaphas and the other authorities—and as we will see shortly, it didn't—but having a populace sympathetic to Christians would provide some margin of safety for Christ's followers.

Bonus Material: The Sadducees

There are many moments, especially in the Gospels, when we read about Pharisees, Sadducees, scribes, Herodians, etc. First-century Judea was a complex society of disparate and overlapping political/religious groups.

Caiaphas was a Sadducee. These Sadducees were the "old guard" of the Hebrews, a sort of religious aristocracy. They lived mainly in Jerusalem and were centered on the Temple traditions, the written Torah, and sacrifices. They did not abide new-fangled ideas like life after death and they did not encourage intellectual debate. The High Priests were generally Sadducees.

Day 12 - Peter Speaks in Solomon's Portico (2)

Acts 3:17-26

"And now, brothers, I know that you acted in ignorance, as did your leaders. But in this way God has fulfilled what He foretold through all the prophets, saying that His Christ would suffer. Repent, then, and turn back, so that your sins may be wiped away, that times of refreshing may come from the presence of the Lord, and that He may send Jesus, the Christ, who has been appointed for you.

Heaven must take Him in until the time comes for the restoration of all things, which God announced long ago through His holy prophets. For Moses said, 'The Lord your God will raise up for you a prophet like me from among your brothers. You must listen to Him in everything He tells you. Everyone who does not listen to Him will be completely cut off from among his people.'

Indeed, all the prophets from Samuel on, as many as have spoken, have proclaimed these days. And you are sons of the prophets and of the covenant God made with your fathers when He said to Abraham, 'Through your offspring all the families of the earth will be blessed.' When God raised up His Servant, He sent Him first to you to bless you by turning each of you from your wicked ways."

Commentary

All of the four gospels recount miracles. In *John* these are given a more focused significance; *John* includes only seven of Christ's miracles and calls them "signs." As we discussed in Day Ten, these are miracles performed specifically to demonstrate that Jesus spoke with the authority of God, by showing that He wielded the supernatural power of God. Miracles had special significance to the first group of converts, who were Jews in Jerusalem, and as Jews, were accustomed to prophets showing their divine credentials by working miracles.

The prophecy of Moses referenced in today's Scripture is, for me, the first explicit prophecy of Christ's coming and one of the most powerfully worded. In Deuteronomy 18:15-22, appearing right in the middle of the mass of laws given by Moses, is a law requiring the Hebrews to honor the Messiah!

Moses predicts the coming of a great prophet, who would be Jewish. God commands the Hebrews to follow the prophet, because he will speak the word of God — if he does not speak the word of God, he shall die. But how, one might wonder, could a confused Jew tell whether the prophet is true — whether he speaks the word of God — or is false and speaking the words of other gods, or the words of demons, or even just speaking his own words?

The answer given in *Deuteronomy* is that, when a prophet speaks in the name of the Lord, if the word does not come to pass or come true, that is a word that the Lord has not spoken. The Messiah (as this great prophet will come to be called) will make <u>accurate</u> predictions. Thus, one significance of Jesus' signs was that they related back to Moses' prophecy. When He told Lazarus to be healed, Lazarus was healed!

Jesus did not perform miracles simply to wow the crowds; He was not a magician putting on a show. Most of His miracles were performed before Jews, many of whom would have known *Deuteronomy* inside-out; for the words of Moses in the Pentateuch were the law by which they were expected to lead their daily lives.

We must remember Jesus' audience. His claims put his listeners in a bind. Much of what he said seemed different from the Jewish Bible, and much of it was directly contradictory to the teachings of the Pharisees, Sadducees, and other Jewish religious leaders. This confounded the listeners; if Jesus was speaking the word of God, they were commanded to listen and follow, but if not, they should ignore Him and possibly put Him to death.

Thus, Jesus' miracles, especially those miracles called "signs" by John, had special significance. When Jesus said something, <u>it came true</u>. Even if it were physically impossible! Because of this, the Jews were able to believe and follow Him, for Moses, the giver of God's law, had told them the Messiah would come and they must follow Him.

Acts 4 – Peter and John Persecuted

Day 13 - Peter and John Arrested

Acts 4:1-12

While Peter and John were speaking to the people, the priests and the captain of the temple guard and the Sadducees came up to them, greatly disturbed that they were teaching the people and proclaiming in Jesus the resurrection of the dead. They seized Peter and John, and because it was evening, they put them in custody until the next day. But many who heard the message believed, and the number of men grew to about five thousand.

The next day the rulers, elders, and scribes assembled in Jerusalem, along with Annas the high priest, Caiaphas, John, Alexander, and many others from the high priest's family. They had Peter and John brought in and began to question them: "By what power or what name did you do this?"

Then Peter, filled with the Holy Spirit, said to them, "Rulers and elders of the people! If we are being examined today about a kind service to a man who was lame, to determine how he was healed, then let this be known to all of you and to all the people of Israel: It is by the name of Jesus Christ of Nazareth, whom you crucified but whom God raised from the dead, that this man stands before you healed.

This Jesus is 'the stone you builders rejected, which has become the cornerstone.' Salvation exists in no one else, for there is no other name under heaven given to men by which we must be saved."

Commentary

Just months after Jesus was tried and executed for heresy, Peter began to preach Jesus' message openly, in public, and right in Jerusalem itself—the heart of the Jewish religious establishment. He has converted 5,000 men. He is practically asking to be arrested and executed.

How far he has come since he denied Jesus three times after Jesus was arrested! (Matthew 26:69-75) Peter is exploding with courage. When Annas and Caiaphas (as well as other high priests) ask him how he has made the lame man whole, Peter gives it to them in spades. He summarizes the very speech he has been making in public to win converts—he even goes so far as to accuse the high priests of murdering a man sent by God.

And then, he tells them right to their faces, that "there is salvation in no one else." They, the high priests, have been superseded. Jesus has replaced the very priests before whom Peter stands. (*See* Hebrews 4:14.)

But the climate has changed. Now, Christians number 5,000 in a city that, by modern standards, is quite small. (Most estimates run about 30,000 to 50,000 permanent residents.) The Sanhedrin must be more careful, because offending so many people would risk a riot. Their strategy of stopping the heresy by executing the leader has failed; this Jesus person has become a real thorn in the Sanhedrin's side.

Bonus Material: Jesus the High Priest

The commentary today about high priests recalls the *Epistle to the Hebrews*, a book of the New Testament which is rather mysterious — nobody knows who wrote it — and unique in its point of view. The "big idea" in *Hebrews* is that Jesus has become the Hebrew high priest.

For example, look at Hebrews 4:14-15: "Therefore, since we have a great high priest who has passed through the heavens, Jesus the Son of God, let us hold firmly to what we profess. For we do not have a high priest who is unable to sympathize with our weaknesses, but we have one who was tempted in every way that we are, yet was without sin."

By extension, Jesus became our high priest; but the concept is more critical to Jews struggling to accept Christ, than to Gentile Christians.

Day 14 - Peter and John on Trial

Acts 4:13-22

When they saw the boldness of Peter and John and realized that they were unschooled, ordinary men, they marveled and took note that these men had been with Jesus. And seeing the man who had been healed standing there with them, they had nothing to say in response. So they ordered them to leave the Sanhedrin and then conferred together.

"What shall we do with these men?" they asked. "It is clear to everyone living in Jerusalem that a remarkable miracle has occurred through them, and we cannot deny it. But to keep this message from spreading any further among the people, we must warn them not to speak to anyone in this name."

Then they called them in again and commanded them not to speak or teach at all in the name of Jesus. But Peter and John replied, "Judge for yourselves whether it is right in God's sight to listen to you rather than God. For we cannot stop speaking about what we have seen and heard."

After further threats they let them go. They could not find a way to punish them, because all the people were glorifying God for what had happened. For the man who was miraculously healed was over forty years old.

Commentary

Caiaphas, Annas, and the rest now have a sticky situation on their hands. Peter and John have openly defied them by teaching the doctrine of Jesus; however, the Sanhedrin cannot discount the miracle, because the healed man is standing right in front of them. Neither can they pass off the miracle as a fraud, because of the man's age, which makes it unlikely that he recovered spontaneously from his lifelong chronic disease. They have to admit it is a "notable sign."

The sentiment against Jesus has begun to shift, which puts the Sanhedrin in an awkward spot. There is no popular hysteria demanding

John and Peter's death; quite the contrary — the number of Jesus' supporters is starting to grow.

They try to strike a bargain with the two apostles: if they will stop preaching, the Sanhedrin will spare their lives. But Peter and John reject it. They are ready to die rather than abandon the mission Christ had left them.

And so the high priests must let them go free — for now.

Bonus Material: Could the Apostles Read and Write?

In today's passage, we learn tangentially that the high priests consider Peter and John to be "unschooled." These were fishermen, blue-collar workers in a time when laborers were generally illiterate.

Matthew might well have been the only apostle who could read and write. In several ways, he appears to be the "odd man out" among the apostles. Eleven of them appear to have been common working men but "good Jews."

Matthew was the opposite. As a tax collector, he was not a very good Jew; he was a Roman collaborator and thus a traitor to his people. But he was educated. Early Christian commentators state that Matthew wrote down Jesus' words in "the Hebrew language," most likely meaning Aramaic, the common language of Judea.

Day 15 - The Believers Pray for Boldness

Acts 4:23-31

On their release, Peter and John returned to their own people and reported everything that the chief priests and elders had said to them. When the believers heard this, they lifted up their voices to God with one accord. "Sovereign Lord," they said, "You made the heaven and the earth and the sea and everything in them. You spoke by the Holy Spirit through the mouth of Your servant, our father David:

'Why do the nations rage
and the peoples plot in vain?

The kings of the earth take their stand
and the rulers gather together
against the Lord
and against His Anointed One.'

In fact, this is the very city where Herod and Pontius Pilate conspired with the Gentiles and the people of Israel against Your holy servant Jesus, whom You anointed. They carried out what Your hand and will had decided beforehand would happen. And now, Lord, consider their threats, and enable Your servants to speak Your word with complete boldness, as You stretch out Your hand to heal and perform signs and wonders through the name of Your holy servant Jesus."

After they had prayed, their meeting place was shaken, and they were all filled with the Holy Spirit and spoke the word of God boldly.

Commentary

Peter and John have just been threatened by the Sanhedrin, in a trial that could have sentenced them to death; they were told not to preach the word of Christ, with the implication that they might be executed, as Jesus himself had been.

They interpret the threat in the light of prophecy, a very specific one made in *Psalm 2*. The "nations" refers to non-Jewish nations, i.e. the Gentiles. (In fact, you might recognize the Hebrew word, *Gôyim.*) Peter and John equate Herod to the many nations that threatened to conquer David's Israel. No surprise there. But they imply that the Sanhedrin —including the high priests of Israel! — have become like foreign powers seeking to destroy God's people.

The psalm predicted exactly what is beginning to happen: the authorities have taken a stand against the Messiah (i.e., "His Anointed One"). In the future, this opposition will spread from Judea throughout the earth, and Christians will be martyred in every land for their beliefs.

They pray for the fortitude to speak Christ's word with confidence; not confidence that they will win over the governments of earth, because the psalm states that the nations will stand against them, but rather confidence in a victory greater than possible among human institutions. And their prayer is answered. They are given heart, through the Holy Spirit, to spread Christ's word against all opposition, without fear.

Their fearlessness is not freedom from fear of harm from other men; they know they will be scorned, reviled, imprisoned, and perhaps even killed. Rather, their courage comes from the certainty that their sacrifice and work is God's will. Their sacrifice will be rewarded for all eternity, and they have already been rewarded by the grace of Christ. Unlike those who do not hear the word and follow Christ, they will be granted perfect peace and eternal life in God's presence.

Application: Boldness in Proclaiming Jesus

The "practical application" of these verses permeates the entire *Book of Acts*, so I will highlight it only once. But I hope you will keep it in mind when reading every chapter.

When we find ourselves reluctant to give testimony about our belief, we might read this passage for encouragement. Why are we reluctant? Do we fear awkwardness, or embarrassment, or perhaps the scorn of anti-Christians, when we share our beliefs with others? Do we think we will sound inarticulate, or stupid?

When we do, it might be helpful to consider all who spoke out their belief in the face of imprisonment, beatings, and execution. I am not advocating that anyone feel ashamed at their own silence. Shame does not generally seem helpful to faith. But it _is_ helpful to seek encouragement to boldness, in God's word.

I can always read about Peter and John, and admire their faith and bravery, even if it is greater than my own. Let us find in them encouragement, rather than shame. Then we will not be reluctant to keep them in mind all of our lives.

Day 16 - Sharing Among the Believers

Acts 4:32-37

The multitude of believers was one in heart and soul. No one claimed that any of his possessions was his own, but they shared everything they owned. With great power the apostles continued to give their testimony about the resurrection of the Lord Jesus. And abundant grace was upon them all.

There were no needy ones among them, because those who owned lands or houses would sell their property, bring the proceeds from the sales, and lay them at the apostles' feet for distribution to anyone as he had need.

Joseph, a Levite from Cyprus, whom the apostles called Barnabas (meaning Son of Encouragement), sold a field he owned, brought the money, and laid it at the apostles' feet.

Commentary

The first followers of Christ practiced an early and extreme form of communal living. All assets were held in common under an agreed leader; those with private property sold it and contributed it to the general fund. Nobody was allowed to go hungry, but it appears that none of them retained any valuable property, such as houses.

It was different from a monastery. People had families; they did not take monastic vows, wear peculiar clothing, live in silence, or have an abbot with total authority. They were so filled with the excitement of the Holy Spirit that they simply did not want to be burdened with property. They automatically adopted Christ's teaching to the man in Matthew 19:21.

Is it a requirement to live like this, to be a "real" Christian? The Bible doesn't really answer the question, although it steers us in that direction. (E.g., Mark 10:17-27.) Love of money, however, is the "root of all evil" (or "all kinds of evil") and this lesson provides a good opportunity for us to examine our own feelings about possessions and money.

Christ promised that God will provide us a basic living. It is helpful to read Matthew 6:19-34 from time to time; it is one of the most important parts of the New Testament.

Craving after expensive possessions is a sin — one that I pray to be forgiven for often! Christ never said that we could not have them. But he clearly said that we could not love them, and he also said that we must look after our poor brethren. If we have food, and clothing, and a warm dry place to live, we should give thanks for it and remember that it is sufficient for earthly happiness.

Acts 5 – The Empty Prison

Day 17 - Ananias and Sapphira

Acts 5:1-11

Now a man named Ananias, together with his wife Sapphira, also sold a piece of property. With his wife's full knowledge, he kept back some of the proceeds for himself, but brought a portion and laid it at the apostles' feet.

Then Peter said, "Ananias, how is it that Satan has filled your heart to lie to the Holy Spirit and withhold some of the proceeds from the land? Did it not belong to you before it was sold? And after it was sold, was it not at your disposal? How could you conceive such a deed in your heart? You have not lied to men, but to God!"

On hearing these words, Ananias fell down and died. And great fear came over all who heard what had happened. Then the young men stepped forward, wrapped up his body, and carried him out and buried him.

About three hours later his wife also came in, unaware of what had happened. "Tell me," said Peter, "is this the price you and your husband got for the land?"

"Yes," she answered, "that is the price."

"How could you agree to test the Spirit of the Lord?" Peter replied. "Look, the feet of the men who buried your husband are at the door, and they will carry you out also."

At that instant she fell down at his feet and died. Then the young men came in and, finding her dead, carried her out and buried her beside her husband. And great fear came over the whole church and all who heard about these events.

Commentary

"Ananias and Sapphira" have become a metaphor for Christian hypocrisy. With the other members of the first church in Jerusalem, they apparently made an oath to the other members, and to God, to sell all that they owned and give the proceeds to the general fund. (The members lived communally— see the previous verses, Acts 4:32-37.) But Ananias and Sapphira did not, and even more importantly, they lied about it.

The Scripture does not say that God caused them to die; very possibly they could have died of sheer shame. Nor did Jesus teach that we would suffer death for not following His word. Just the opposite, in fact; He told the disciples that many of them would suffer physical death for following and spreading His teachings.

What, then, are we to make of this passage? <u>We should not lie to God</u>.

It is human nature to try to make ourselves look good, to arrange the facts of our lives so that we seem righteous. If we argue with our spouse or a coworker, how often we will rehearse the facts in our mind, remembering why the other person was at fault and why we were justified in arguing.

But rehearsing our self-righteousness is sinful pride, operating at full force. We do not find salvation in our own righteousness, but by the grace of God. Here's a trivia question for you: What is the first thing Jesus tells us to do in the New Testament?

Answer: Repent! (Mark 1:15)

<u>Application Question:</u>

How do we harm our Godly mission by trying to make ourselves look good to others? Why do we do it? How about trying to look good to ourselves, i.e. seeking self-esteem?

Day 18 - The Apostles Heal Many (Peter's Shadow)

Acts 5:12-16

The apostles performed many signs and wonders among the people, and with one accord the believers gathered together in Solomon's Colonnade. Although the people regarded them highly, no one else dared to join them. Yet more and more believers were brought to the Lord—large numbers of both men and women.

As a result, people brought the sick into the streets and laid them on cots and mats, so that at least Peter's shadow might fall on some of them as he passed by. Crowds also gathered from the towns around Jerusalem, bringing the sick and those tormented by unclean spirits, and all of them were healed.

Commentary

From the moment of Christ's Resurrection, the courage of Christ's followers has risen slowly. What Caiaphas and the Sanhedrin feared is coming to pass. The apostles teach and heal openly, both in the streets of the city and on Solomon's porch — the very eastern portico of the Temple of Jerusalem, the holiest place in Judaism and the seat of the Sanhedrin. The apostles realize they might be arrested and executed, but they nevertheless spread Christ's word with vigor.

Peter's fame as the founder of the church has become established. As they did with Jesus, people gather in the streets hoping simply that his shadow will fall upon them. This is symbolic of St. Peter's legacy; for the church that he founds will survive, to save those who become members, after his body has died. As we say today, "he cast a long shadow."

Word of Christ's Resurrection and the new church in Jerusalem has escalated. People have begun to flood into Jerusalem from the areas around it. The Holy Spirit is spreading like a wildfire, emanating from a central point in an expanding ring of righteousness.

Many of these earliest converts are the physically and mentally ill, which reflects Christ's teaching in the Sermon on the Mount, especially the Beatitudes (Matthew 5:1-12). The poor in spirit, the most humble and meek, are the first to be blessed. Their physical illness is symbolic of the spiritual illness that has infected the world since the time of Adam, and so their healing symbolizes their spiritual salvation.

Day 19 - The Apostles Arrested Again

Acts 5:17-21

Then the high priest and all his associates, who belonged to the party of the Sadducees, were filled with jealousy. They went out and arrested the apostles and put them in the public jail. But during the night an angel of the Lord opened the doors of the jail and brought them out, saying, "Go, stand in the temple courts and tell the people the full message of this new life."

At daybreak the apostles entered the temple courts as they had been told and began to teach the people.

Commentary

There were two great Jewish political/religious parties in Judea, the Sadducees (see *Day 11*) and the Pharisees. The Sadducees were much like the early Hebrews, emphasizing ritual (such as sacrifice); they were centered in Jerusalem. The priests tended to be Sadducees.

The equally powerful Pharisees put more emphasis on interpreting God's word and theology (similar to modern-day Judaism) and were more dispersed throughout Judea. Their leaders were more like "rabbis," and they were popular among devout Jews. But despite their enmity towards one another, both groups wanted to kill Jesus and his followers.

(One might say there was a third political party, the Herodians, who were basically Roman collaborators and were hardly "Jewish" at all; they did not seem to play much part in the Sanhedrin and, unlike the Pharisees and Sadducees, were not secretly hoping for the end Roman occupation and rule. But they did not like Jesus or the Christians either.)

The Sadducees got to Peter and his followers first. They arrested them and put them in prison; presumably, they intended to try them and execute them. But, unlike Christ, the apostles are not intended to be God's sacrifice; they are intended to go into the world and preach.

Their story still has notable parallels to Christ's. The authorities had them arrested, as they had arrested Christ. And as with Christ, God steps in to show that the world has no real power over them. They are "reborn" in a sense, because they defeat the prison of sin and go free.

Day 20 - The Empty Prison

Acts 5:21-26

At daybreak the apostles entered the temple courts as they had been told and began to teach the people.

When the high priest and his associates arrived, they convened the Sanhedrin—the full assembly of the elders of Israel—and sent to the jail for the apostles. But on arriving at the jail, the officers did not find them there. So they returned with the report: "We found the jail securely locked, with the guards posted at the doors; but when we opened them, we found no one inside."

When the captain of the temple guard and the chief priests heard this account, they were perplexed as to what was happening. Then someone came in and announced, "Look, the men you put in jail are standing in the temple courts teaching the people!"

At that point, the captain went with the officers and brought the apostles—but not by force, for fear the people would stone them.

Commentary

Don't you just want to say "Ha! Take that!" to the high priest and the Sanhedrin? The time of miracles is still with the apostles, and it will continue (although perhaps diminishing) for several years. During that time, the theme of defeating prison, which relates to Christ defeating death, will reoccur several times.

Our prison is our mortal self. Just as physical stones can prevent a person from physically moving outside a wall, so our body—and our "physical" mind, which is part of our body—can keep us from moving towards God and hold us, forcibly, inside the world we can see and touch.

If you doubt that our minds are part of our bodies, think of this example: Imagine a person standing on a ledge 1000 feet in the air. There is no wind and the person is healthy and has such good balance that he can snow ski skillfully. Will this person feel giddy? Almost certainly. (I have walked out on the Skywalk of the Grand Canyon, a transparent walkway thousands of feet above the jagged rocks of the canyon floor, and I could barely bring myself to move!)

Our human mind is hard-wired to our physical body. If a young heterosexual man sees a beautiful woman in a bikini, he will be aroused even against his will. If someone points a loaded shotgun in our faces, our hearts will beat faster. If someone insults us, we get angry, even if we can suppress it.

But God's Holy Spirit can ameliorate and even overcome our physical mind, given time and prayer. Thousands of Christians have faced death without apparent fear, singing hymns and praising God. Their courage, in fact, was one of the primary historical reasons for the rapid growth of Christianity in the first few centuries after Christ died. It is one of the great lessons of the resurrection. God can and will overcome the greatest power of the world, the power of death.

We can thus overcome sin, at least in great part. The Bible promises this to us: "The temptations in your life are no different from what others experience. And God is faithful. He will not allow the temptation to be more than you can stand. When you are tempted, he will show you a way out so that you can endure." (1 Corinthians 10:13)

Just as a prison of stone walls cannot hold Peter's body, the prison of our mortal selves cannot hold our souls in captivity. The laws of the physical world ultimately crumble before the power of Almighty God.

Notice that the guards are afraid to take the apostles by force; the apostles, however, show no fear at all. Immediately upon their release, they return to the activity for which they were being tried: teaching at the temple. Christian belief has spread quickly, to the point that the greatest human power on earth, the soldiers of the Roman Empire, become cautious.

Bonus Discussion: The Shame or Guilt of Sin

I feel called to add something. I counsel innumerable people, especially young people, who think that, because they have a persistent sin, that they have lost their faith or their faith is insufficient for their salvation. They get depressed by terrible feelings of shame or guilt.

It seems most often to concern sex (activity, or desires, or pornography, and so on) but it can be anything: prayer life, money, fighting, times of wavering faith. Anything.

Do not fall into this trap! Repeat after me: "If we confess our sins, he is faithful and just and will forgive us our sins and purify us from all unrighteousness." (1 John 1:9) Tattoo this on your arm if you have to.

Satan wants you to doubt your salvation. God does not. God is faithful. God loves you. If you confess your sin, He will forgive you.

Your church may have a specific format for confession. Whatever your belief, make sure you have confidence in the result. Live your life in the joy of your salvation in Christ!!

Day 21 - The Council Chastises Peter

Acts 5:27-32

They brought them in and made them stand before the Sanhedrin, where the high priest interrogated them. "We gave you strict orders not to teach in this name," he said. "Yet you have filled Jerusalem with your teaching and are determined to make us responsible for this man's blood."

But Peter and the other apostles replied, "We must obey God rather than men. The God of our fathers raised up Jesus, whom you had killed by hanging Him on a tree. God exalted Him to His right hand as Prince and Savior, in order to grant repentance and forgiveness of sins to Israel. We are witnesses of these things, and so is the Holy Spirit, whom God has given to those who obey Him."

Commentary

This time, it is not just Peter and John who appear for trial, but all the apostles. The Jewish authorities again display the hypocrisy which they showed so clearly at Christ's Crucifixion. They try to avoid their responsibility for the crucifixion of Jesus and become angry at those who tell the truth.

The apostles, however, will have none of it. They know who was truly responsible for Jesus' crucifixion, and they hold the high priests themselves accountable for it. Saying this in open court would have shocked the high priests, with its insolence. And furthermore, having been arrested for claiming that Christ was the Son of God, they have the nerve to preach their message right to the high priests themselves.

The apostles have become utterly brazen in the face of death. Their faith is beyond reproach. And may we all become like them, ready to witness to Christ's miracle in any situation, no matter how hostile it may be.

This also brings up two knotty problems. First, Paul tells us repeatedly to submit ourselves to the governing authorities, yet here is Peter himself, defying them. The answer is to differentiate between the civil government — earthly authority — and religious authorities. We obey God, and God has told us to obey whatever government rules us. But when authorities directly contradict a duty God has placed upon us, we must disobey them. But note and note well: Peter and the apostles are not engaging in political rebellion; they place themselves in the hands of the council for whatever punishment their actions might deserve.

Much harder to understand is Paul's statement in Romans 13. He tells us, in a nutshell, that the authorities are instituted by God to punish wrongdoing. While this is basically impossible to reconcile intellectually, it is easy enough to follow in practice. We must obey the civil law unless it directly contradicts a God-given duty, and when we must disobey it, we must accept our punishment.

Why must we treat the judgments of evil men, who have seized earthly power, as if they were God's servants? I don't know. It is some help to remember that the Sanhedrin was doing God's will by crucifying Jesus.

But mostly, I understand that God and His word are beyond my comprehension. It is foolishness, not logic, that brings us salvation. "For Christ did not send me [Paul] to baptize but to preach the gospel, and not with words of eloquent wisdom, lest the cross of Christ be emptied of its power." (1 Cor. 1:17-31)

And as a final word on this difficult issue, let us repeat the teaching in Acts 5:29 – "We must obey God rather than men."

Discussion Question: When Must We Obey the Government?

A productive discussion question jumps out at us, in light of the difficulties reconciling Romans 13 and Acts 5. When must we obey the governing authorities, and when must we disobey? What other Scripture speaks to this dichotomy?

We will see a related issue in Acts 23:5, when Paul asserts "You shall not speak evil of a ruler of your people."

Day 22 - The Honor of Punishment

Acts 5:33-42

When the Council members heard this, they were enraged, and they resolved to put the apostles to death. But a Pharisee named Gamaliel, a teacher of the law who was honored by all the people, stood up in the Sanhedrin and ordered that the men be put outside for a short time.

"Men of Israel," he said, "consider carefully what you are about to do to these men. Some time ago Theudas rose up, claiming to be somebody, and about four hundred men joined him. He was killed, all his followers were dispersed, and it all came to nothing. After him, Judas the Galilean appeared in the days of the census and drew away people after him. He too perished, and all his followers were scattered.

So in the present case I advise you: Leave these men alone. Let them go! For if their purpose or endeavor is of human origin, it will fail. But if it is from God, you will not be able to stop them. You may even find yourselves fighting against God."

At this, they yielded to Gamaliel. They called the apostles in and had them flogged. Then they ordered them not to speak in the name of Jesus, and released them.

The apostles left the Sanhedrin, rejoicing that they had been counted worthy of suffering disgrace for the Name. Every day, in the temple courts and from house to house, they did not stop teaching and proclaiming the good news that Jesus is the Christ.

Commentary

The high priests are not accustomed to defiance. Like most men, power has corrupted them and made them proud. The insolence of the apostles makes them angry and their anger, in addition to the merits of the case, impels them to kill the apostles immediately.

But a cooler head prevails. Gamaliel, showing the reason for his fame, makes an excellent point. If Christianity represents nothing but a deviant sect, history predicts that it will simply die out. But if the apostles are preaching God's will, the high priests — whose duty is, after all, not to protect their own power, but to guard the word of God — should not be suppressing them. Like many Pharisees (and perhaps even Pilate), he is willing to entertain their theology and the possibility that Jesus was a prophet.

So, for a second time, the apostles get off with a warning (although this one includes a whipping — and beatings in those days were severe). But even with the physical punishment, we see the apostles' courage and faith grow yet another step.

After the trial, they must have realized that they were facing execution; however, not only do they appear to be unafraid of death, but also, they rejoice that they had been allowed to be flogged in the service of Christ! They embody Christ's words, "Greater love hath no man than this, that a man lay down his life for his friends." (John 15:13)

The Christ sect continues to gather steam. It has grown from 120 to 5,000 adherents in Jerusalem, and people are starting to come to Jerusalem from the countryside just to be part of it.

Acts 6 – The Early Church

Day 23 - Governing the Early Church

Acts 6:1-7

In those days when the disciples were increasing in number, the Grecian Jews among them began to grumble against the Hebraic Jews because their widows were being overlooked in the daily distribution of food.

So the Twelve summoned all the disciples and said, "It is unacceptable for us to neglect the word of God in order to wait on tables. Therefore, brothers, select from among you seven men confirmed to be full of the Spirit and wisdom. We will appoint this responsibility to them and will devote ourselves to prayer and to the ministry of the word."

This proposal pleased the whole group. They chose Stephen, a man full of faith and of the Holy Spirit, as well as Philip, Prochorus, Nicanor, Timon, Parmenas, and Nicolas from Antioch, a convert to Judaism. They presented these seven to the apostles, who prayed and laid their hands on them.

So the word of God continued to spread. The number of disciples in Jerusalem grew rapidly, and a great number of priests became obedient to the faith.

Commentary

If you have ever belonged to a church, this should sound familiar; it is the first recorded dispute in church politics. The Hellenists were not Gentile Greeks, but Jews who had lived outside Judea long enough to adopt the Greek language and culture. They were readily accepted into the church, but they were "different" from the native Israelites.

Saying that their widows were not being served was a serious matter. Women did not own land and widows often had to earn their food by gleaning fallen grain from fields that had been harvested—hard work for little reward. Taking care of widows was a very big deal. (*Cf.* 1 Timothy 5:3-16, where Paul writes an entire essay on ministry to widows!)

"Wait on tables," in this passage, does not refer to cooking, serving, and cleaning up after meals. Rather it refers to sitting at the table conducting church business. It might mean physically dispensing food; most likely it includes handling money, accounting, and so on. Those who served at the table were the first vestry or perhaps deacons. (Philip, who appears prominently in later chapters of *Acts*, is sometimes called "Philip the Deacon.")

So the dispute was resolved, basically, by putting Hellenists in charge of practical things. The apostles had no lust for power; just the opposite. They gave the Hellenists the power to decide how and to whom food would be served. The apostles were more needed out in the field converting new members, not in the home office. Would that intra-church political disputes were always settled in this spirit today, following Christ's command that "if a man asks you for your coat, give him your cloak also." (Matthew 5:40)

In a general election, seven of the Hellenists are elected. Seven, because that was the customary number of men who served as the local council of a Jewish community — it was what they were accustomed to. Christianity was still very much a Jewish sect. (And notice that all of the seven have Greek names.)

The apostles were not loath to work in addition to their preaching. Many of them must have supported themselves during their ministry; we know, for example, that Paul made tents in order to support himself on his journeys. Rather, it was a matter of allocating resources: the apostles were most needed out in the streets, spreading the gospel, bringing in new members, or spending their time in prayer and teaching.

But notice, the men chosen from the Hellenists were no less filled with the Holy Spirit than the Hebrew Christians. We are introduced here to (St.) Stephen, a man of such enormous importance to Christianity that more than two chapters of the Bible are devoted to his story, beginning with tomorrow's lesson. And as stated above, we will encounter Philip (the Deacon) several times later in *Acts*.

Bonus Discussion: The Hellenists

Think for a second about how many different cultures include Christians. A woman in a village in Kenya, or a Chinese farmer, might have the identical beliefs about Christ as you, despite huge differences in culture and language. The same situation applies to the Hellenists. They were Jews who were devout and fully Jewish by religion, but Egyptian or Macedonian or Roman in culture.

In the 500 years before Christ, the Jews were repeatedly dispersed from Canaan until they lived in every corner of the empires which had conquered them, particularly the Persian, Macedonian, and Roman Empires. So, when the early Christians gathered into tight-knit communities, first in Jerusalem and later in other places, tensions inevitably arose between the Aramaic-speaking Jews of Judea and the Hellenists. We will see other difficulties in later chapters.

Hellenistic Jews were a powerful force in Judaism. As we previously mentioned, the first complete "Hebrew" Bible (called the *Septuagint*) was written in Greek and compiled in Egypt.

The Jews, then and now, call their Bible the *Tanakh*. This is more or less identical to our Old Testament. So the *Septuagint* was the first *Tanakh*.

In case you are not sufficiently confused yet, the first five book of the *Tanakh* are called the *Pentateuch* by Christians and the *Torah* by Jews. And the Jews also have a holy book called the *Talmud*, which is a collection of rabbinic teachings and commentaries on the *Tanakh*.

Day 24 - Stephen is Seized

Acts 6:8-15

Now Stephen, who was full of grace and power, was performing great wonders and signs among the people. But resistance arose from what was called the Synagogue of the Freedmen, including Cyrenians, Alexandrians, and men from the provinces of Cilicia and Asia. They began to argue with Stephen, but they could not stand up to his wisdom or the Spirit by whom he spoke.

Then they prompted some men to say, "We heard Stephen speak words of blasphemy against Moses and against God."

So they stirred up the people, elders, and scribes and confronted Stephen. They seized him and brought him before the Sanhedrin, where they presented false witnesses who said, "This man never stops speaking against this holy place and against the law. For we have heard him say that Jesus of Nazareth will destroy this place and change the customs that Moses handed down to us."

All who were sitting in the Sanhedrin looked intently at Stephen, and they saw that his face was like the face of an angel.

Commentary

Stephen is soon to become the first martyr in Christianity. Not much is known about him. He was probably the Greek Jew named in yesterday's lesson, who was appointed (possibly as the leader) to the group who would oversee administration of the Jerusalem church. He was noted to be a man filled with the Holy Spirit and likely stood out in his faith and zeal — which would explain why he was singled out.

Does the phrase "full of grace and power" ring a bell? It is a description applied to Jesus. (John 1:14)

The groups who line up against him are all foreigners, people who, like Stephen himself, had returned to Jerusalem after the first diaspora. Cyrenia was an important city in Libya and Alexandria was, of course, in Egypt. Cilicia and "Asia" were the area around Turkey and Greece. The Freedmen were a group of former slaves.

So one might guess that Stephen, being a foreigner himself and speaking excellent Greek, would have spent time converting these groups. It would explain why they were the ones bringing charges against him.

The expression "face like an angel" does not mean he was unusually handsome. Rather, he was so filled with the Holy Spirit that his face shone with inspiration. His defense, which makes up the entirety of

Acts 7, shows a skill at oratory that reminds us of a promise: "And when they bring you before the synagogues and the rulers and the authorities, do not be anxious about how you should defend yourself or what you should say, for the Holy Spirit will teach you in that very hour what you ought to say." (Luke 12:11-12)

Application Question: Honoring the Humble Servant

Notice that Stephen was one of the seven chosen to handle more mundane affairs in the church, because the Twelve were "too busy to wait on tables." Yet Stephen will be forever glorified as the first martyr to Christ.

How often do we glorify those who teach, write, or lead more than those who serve more "humble" roles? Is this God's will?

The pride and even arrogance of leadership is an enormously destructive force in Christianity. How can we ameliorate the problem without becoming angry or judgmental?

Acts 7 – Stephen is Martyred

Day 25 - Stephen's Speech to the Sanhedrin (1)

Acts 7:1-8

Then the high priest asked Stephen, "Are these charges true?"

And Stephen declared: "Brothers and fathers, listen to me! The God of glory appeared to our father Abraham while he was still in Mesopotamia, before he lived in Haran, and told him, 'Leave your country and your kindred and go to the land I will show you.' So Abraham left the land of the Chaldeans and settled in Haran. After his father died, God brought him out of that place and into this land where you are now living.

He gave him no inheritance here, not even a foot of ground. But God promised to give possession of the land to Abraham and his descendants, even though he did not yet have a child. God told him that his descendants would be foreigners in a strange land, and that they would be enslaved and mistreated four hundred years. 'But I will punish the nation that enslaves them,' God said, 'and afterward they will come forth and worship Me in this place.'

Then God gave Abraham the covenant of circumcision, and Abraham became the father of Isaac and circumcised him on the eighth day. And Isaac became the father of Jacob, and Jacob of the twelve patriarchs."

Commentary

At this juncture—in the New Testament, after the Gospels—we might be surprised to get a basic history of Judaism. Stephen, in his defense before the Sanhedrin, gives us the CliffsNotes version of Hebrew History.

But the history recap is useful. The Old Testament is so long and full of details that the broad outline can be difficult to grasp. And also, such a summary belongs in the Bible, because there is no primary source for it outside the Bible. The early Hebrews (before David) were inconsequential to the rest of the ancient world. There is no secular mention of them other than a single line on an Egyptian stela (an inscribed stone slab) from 1200 B.C.

Bonus Material: The Bible and Archaeology

The more time passes, the more evidence archaeologists find of events previously known only from the Old Testament. A recent example: Most secular historians thought King David was a myth until 1993, when an ancient tablet was dug up in Northern Israel, providing historical evidence of David and his kingdom.

The great Hittite Empire was unknown outside the Bible until the 19th century. Many secular scholars thought that it was fabricated! They cited the "make believe" Hittites to prove that the Bible was fictional; yet, time has shown the opposite. Discovery of Hittite ruins gave the Bible credibility.

We also know, from archaeological evidence, that the journey of Abraham was plausible. Genesis 11:31 recounts that Abraham left "Ur of the Chaldees" and traveled to "Harran," a journey which Stephen reiterates in today's Scripture. Ur — an ancient Sumerian city — was discovered by archaeologists in 1862.

Harran still exists today. It is a small town in Turkey which was settled as a trading outpost of Ur roughly two thousand years before Christ. So, there would have been traffic between them in 2000 B.C.

Harran may actually be the oldest continuously inhabited town in the world, although most votes go to another Biblical town: Jericho.

Day 26 - Stephen's Speech to the Sanhedrin (2)

Acts 7:9-22

Because the patriarchs were jealous of Joseph, they sold him as a slave into Egypt. But God was with him and rescued him from all his troubles. He granted Joseph favor and wisdom in the sight of Pharaoh king of Egypt, who appointed him ruler over Egypt and all his household.

Then famine and great suffering swept across Egypt and Canaan, and our fathers could not find food. When Jacob heard that there was grain in Egypt, he sent our fathers on their first visit. On their second visit, Joseph revealed his identity to his brothers, and his family became known to Pharaoh. Then Joseph sent for his father Jacob and all his relatives, seventy-five in all.

So Jacob went down to Egypt, where he and our fathers died. Their bones were carried back to Shechem and placed in the tomb that Abraham had bought from the sons of Hamor at Shechem for a price he paid in silver.

As the time drew near for God to fulfill His promise to Abraham, our people in Egypt increased greatly in number. Then another king, who knew nothing of Joseph, arose over Egypt. He exploited our people and oppressed our fathers, forcing them to abandon their infants so they would die.

At that time Moses was born, and he was beautiful in the sight of God. For three months he was nurtured in his father's house. When he was set outside, Pharaoh's daughter took him and brought him up as her own son. So Moses was educated in all the wisdom of the Egyptians and was powerful in speech and action.

Commentary

Today's Scripture is a continuation of Stephen's defense before the Sanhedrin. We have had to break Stephen's speech up, simply because it is so long. In this part, Stephen recounts how the Hebrews came to live in Egypt and then became slaves of the Pharaoh.

Stephen not only recites a summary of early Hebrew history, but he also makes some sense of it that we might not get from reading the Pentateuch. We know that the very early Hebrew history was not written until long after it had happened, especially Genesis 1-11: the Creation, Adam and Eve, Noah, etc. Until about 1900 B.C., the only writing known was Egyptian hieroglyphs. The first alphabet (the Proto-Sinaitic) and thus the first modern writing appeared in Canaan sometime between 1900 B.C. and 1200 B.C., roughly consistent with the time of the Hebrew exodus from Egypt.

Stephen's account of this period emphasizes Moses' role as a scholar. He would have learned hieroglyphic writing if he "learned everything Egyptian wisdom had to offer." Many scholars trace the origins of the Phoenician-Semitic alphabet to hieroglyphics. Thus, it is entirely possible that Moses, coming into Canaan from Egypt, brought writing with him, enabling Hebrew scholars to write down the oral traditions that had been handed down for countless centuries, from Jewish parents and teachers to their children.

Bonus Material: the Phoenician-Semitic alphabet

Just as a matter of interest, the Phoenician-Semitic alphabet was a distant predecessor of the modern English alphabet. You can see a number of similarities, and even more so if you know any Greek letters. Just rotate the D or K to get delta or kappa!

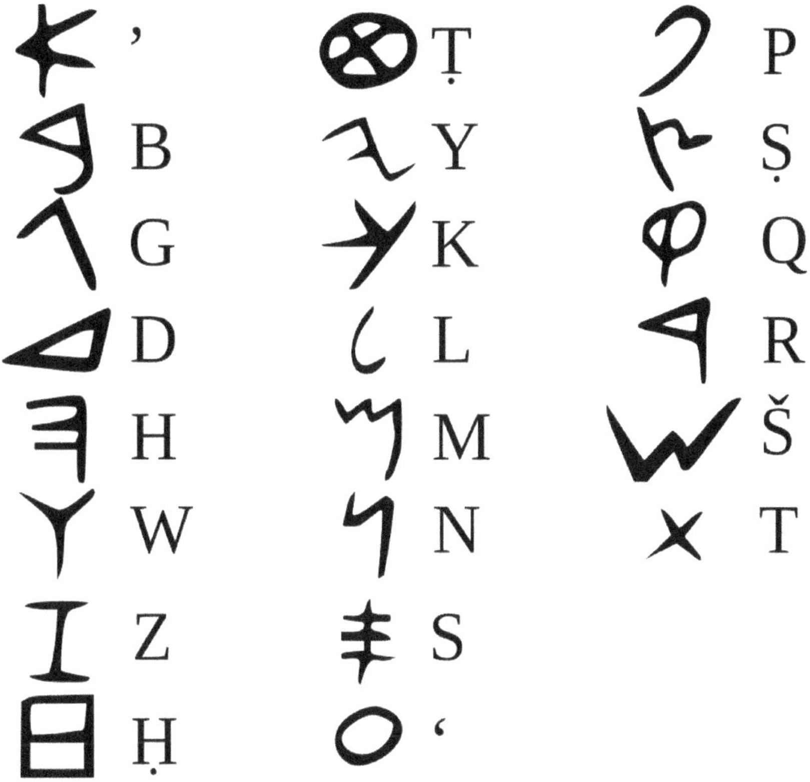

Day 27 - Stephen's Speech to the Sanhedrin (3)

Acts 7:23-32

When Moses was forty years old, he decided to visit his brothers, the children of Israel. And when he saw one of them being mistreated, Moses went to his defense and avenged him by striking down the Egyptian who was oppressing him. He assumed his brothers would understand that God was using him to deliver them, but they did not.

The next day he came upon two Israelites who were fighting, and he tried to reconcile them, saying, 'Men, you are brothers. Why are you mistreating each other?'

But the man who was abusing his neighbor pushed Moses aside and said, 'Who made you ruler and judge over us? Do you want to kill me as you killed the Egyptian yesterday?' At this remark, Moses fled to the land of Midian, where he lived as a foreigner and had two sons.

After forty years had passed, an angel appeared to Moses in the flames of a burning bush in the desert near Mount Sinai. When Moses saw it, he marveled at the sight. As he approached to look more closely, the voice of the Lord came to him: 'I am the God of your fathers, the God of Abraham, Isaac, and Jacob.' Moses trembled with fear and did not dare to look.

Commentary

This is a continuation of Stephen's defense of himself before the Sanhedrin, and there isn't much to say about it. Today's lesson is simply a summary of a passage from *Exodus*.

The short introductory verse, though, has a life lesson that is hard to learn. Many (most?) of us have difficulty taking instruction and correction. It may involve some childhood situation or even trauma, or it may seem to have been born with us; it may spring from rebelliousness, or from a simple lack of trust; but it always involves the sin of pride.

Our pride defeats us. (Proverbs 11:2) For which of us would willingly do worse, when we could do better? But we must learn: God disciplines those He loves. (Revelation 3:19; Proverbs 3:11-12)

Remember the story of the rich young ruler? (Matthew 19:16-26) We never learned if he followed Christ's instructions to give away his money, but the text did tell us that the man was unhappy at the advice to give away all he possessed! "But when the young man heard this statement, he went away grieving; for he was one who owned much property." (Matthew 19:22)

We must confess, we must ask for forgiveness; and sometimes we must also accept instruction and correction, which is the hard part. (Proverbs 28:13; 1 John 1:9) Otherwise, our pride will make it impossible for us to follow God's will. (Hebrews 12:11)

Day 28 - Stephen's Speech to the Sanhedrin (4)

Acts 7:35-43

This Moses, whom they had rejected with the words, 'Who made you ruler and judge?' is the one whom God sent to be their ruler and redeemer through the angel who appeared to him in the bush. He led them out and performed wonders and signs in the land of Egypt, at the Red Sea, and for forty years in the wilderness.

This is the same Moses who told the Israelites, 'God will raise up for you a prophet like me from among your brothers.' He was in the assembly in the wilderness with the angel who spoke to him on Mount Sinai, and with our fathers. And he received living words to pass on to us.

But our fathers refused to obey him. Instead, they rejected him and in their hearts turned back to Egypt. They said to Aaron, 'Make us gods who will go before us! As for this Moses who led us out of the land of Egypt, we do not know what has happened to him.'

At that time they made a calf and offered a sacrifice to the idol, rejoicing in the works of their hands. But God turned away from them and gave them over to the worship of the host of heaven, as it is written in the book of the prophets:

'Did you bring Me sacrifices and offerings
forty years in the wilderness, O house of Israel?

You have taken along the tabernacle of Molech
and the star of your god Rephan,
the idols you made to worship.

Therefore I will send you into exile
beyond Babylon.'"

Commentary

The purpose of Stephen's long speech to the Sanhedrin begins to take shape. Although it sounds like a simple synopsis of Hebrew history, we start to hear an emphasis on the Hebrews' repeated refusals to worship God or follow His prophets.

It is becoming clear that Stephen has no interest in proving his "innocence" of the charge against him; he is accused of preaching the divinity of Christ and he will not deny it. Instead, he is doing exactly what he is accused of! He is lecturing the Sanhedrin on Christ's divinity, but doing it in a gradual way, so that they will not force him to stop talking. He wants them to hear the entire argument he has in mind to deliver to them.

He outlines the disobedience of the Hebrews to Moses and their unwillingness to accept a prophet who had been sent by God. He shows the consequences that flowed from that disobedience, i.e. a return to slavery under a foreign power. And finally, he recounts the prophecy given by Moses, that God would raise up a future prophet from among their people.

He is, in short, reminding them that the word of God is a living thing and that God could send a new prophet with a new and improved Message.

In all fairness, the religious authorities of Judea were sometimes devout men; they were not the idol worshippers who opposed Moses. And yet, Stephen is essentially comparing them to such idol worshippers, because they have refused to recognize the Messiah prophesied by Moses.

Day 29 - Stephen's Speech to the Sanhedrin (5)

Acts 7:44-53

Our fathers had the tabernacle of the Testimony with them in the wilderness. It was constructed exactly as God had directed Moses, according to the pattern he had seen. And our fathers who received it brought it in with Joshua when they dispossessed the nations God drove out before them. It remained until the time of David, who found favor in the sight of God and asked to provide a dwelling place for the God of Jacob. But it was Solomon who built the house for Him.

However, the Most High does not dwell in houses made by human hands. As the prophet says:

> 'Heaven is My throne
> and the earth is My footstool.
> What kind of house will you build for Me, says the
> Lord,
> or where will My place of repose be?
> Has not My hand made all these things?'

You stiff-necked people with uncircumcised hearts and ears! You always resist the Holy Spirit, just as your fathers did. Which of the prophets did your fathers fail to persecute? They even killed those who foretold the coming of the Righteous One. And now you are His betrayers and murderers - you who received the law ordained by angels, yet have not kept it."

Commentary

Stephen has been arrested by the Sanhedrin for preaching the gospel in Jerusalem, after the apostles (and others) have been previously arrested, warned, and flogged. He is making his defense before them. In the previous verses, the beginning of his speech simply summarized the history of the Hebrews. But now, his speech begins to show some teeth.

First, he proves that God does not dwell in a building. (Something we might well remember!) This is a slap in the face to the Jewish authorities. The Sanhedrin is packed with Sadducees, the Jewish politi-cal/religious party that emphasizes worship in the great Temple and the necessity of making the sacrifices. They are very oriented toward "God in a building."

But Christ has taken God out of the Temple and put him into the hearts of the people. The earthly city of Jerusalem— "the present-day Jerusalem," as Paul terms it in Galatians 4:25—is no longer the city of God; it has become the city of slavery.

Having affronted the Sadducees, he then attacks the Pharisees. The Jews circumcised male children as a mandatory symbol of their devo-tion to God, under the Old Covenant. But it was only a symbol. By saying that they are not circumcised in their heart and ears, Stephen is calling them hypocrites; they follow the outward ceremonies of wor-ship, but do not have God in their hearts. Particularly, their "ears" are closed to the word of God. (Compare Galatians 5:2, when Paul tells Gentiles, "If you receive circumcision, Christ will be of no benefit to you.")

Stephen then recounts the history of other such men, who have slain the prophets. In particular, they have killed the prophets who pre-dicted the coming of a Messiah. The prophets delivered God's message, but the Jewish authorities refused to listen.

This is quite a defense. Instead of seeking acquittal of the charges against him, he attacks the judges; it is they, not he, who will be judged under the laws by which they accuse him.

Day 30 - The Stoning of Stephen

Acts 7:54-60

On hearing this, the members of the Sanhedrin were enraged, and they gnashed their teeth at him. But Stephen, full of the Holy Spirit, looked intently into heaven and saw the glory of God and Jesus stand-ing at the right hand of God. "Look," he said, "I see heaven open and the Son of Man standing at the right hand of God."

At this they covered their ears, cried out in a loud voice, and rushed together at him. They dragged him out of the city and began to stone him. Meanwhile the witnesses laid their garments at the feet of a young man named Saul.

While they were stoning him, Stephen appealed, "Lord Jesus, receive my spirit." Falling on his knees, he cried out in a loud voice, "Lord, do not hold this sin against them." And when he had said this, he fell asleep.

Commentary

When we reach the end of the moving story of Stephen, the parallel to the life and crucifixion of Jesus becomes clear. In Acts 6, Stephen was seized for heresy and dragged before the Sanhedrin. The entirety of Acts 7 recounts his lengthy defense.

Stephen first told the story of the Hebrews from Abraham to David, to show that their history was a preparation for the coming of a Messiah. He then accused the Sanhedrin, made up of the mightiest and highest-ranking religious authorities of Judea, of killing God! He compares them to the wicked Hebrew leaders who had killed prophets throughout Jewish history.

Even worse, he testifies that the Temple itself is no longer a holy place, that God no longer dwells in it. And the men in charge of it — those judging him — have lost any claim to righteousness.

Stephens's defense makes such a terrible accusation that the high priests cannot even stand to hear it. They lose control. They cover their ears, they gnash their teeth, and they beat him to death with stones.

Stephen thus becomes the first great Christian martyr. In all Christendom, he is studied as the great model of Christian virtue, a model for many to come; in the Catholic and Orthodox churches, and the more liturgical Protestant communions, he is venerated as a saint.

Do not miss the reference to a young minion named Saul, who holds the high priests' cloaks while they rush out to kill Stephen. We shall see a great deal more of him shortly!

If you wonder why this chapter is so long, remember that Luke — whose mission as a writer so closely intertwined with Paul's ministry —

wrote primarily for the Gentiles. So, this long recap of the Old Testament was many readers' first exposure to the story of Abraham and Moses, the background of human salvation.

Acts 8 – Saul, Peter, Philip

Day 31 - Saul Ravages the Church

Acts 8:1-8

And Saul was there, giving approval to Stephen's death.

On that day a great persecution broke out against the church in Jerusalem, and all except the apostles were scattered throughout Judea and Samaria. God-fearing men buried Stephen and mourned deeply over him. But Saul began to destroy the church. Going from house to house, he dragged off men and women and put them in prison.

Those who had been scattered preached the word wherever they went. Philip went down to a city in Samaria and proclaimed the Christ to them. The crowds gave their undivided attention to Philip's message and to the signs they saw him perform. With loud shrieks, unclean spirits came out of many who were possessed, and many of the paralyzed and lame were healed. So there was great joy in that city.

Commentary

The first great figure in *Acts* has been Peter. We are now introduced to the second, Saul. (He will rename himself "Paul" and dominate the second half of *Acts*.) In the previous verses, he was the man who held the high priests' cloaks, while they ran after Stephen and stoned him to death in a rage. Lest we be unsure, today's reading states bluntly that he "approved" of Stephen's murder. So Saul was a dedicated underling; an apprentice to the priesthood of the Temple, a young man making his way up the ladder of Pharisee hypocrisy.

And Saul shines in his ambition; he shows no qualms about becoming an accessory to murder. The high priests have previously been circumspect in their treatment of the Christian heretics, letting them off with warnings and beatings. But Stephen's outrageous speech during his trial was the last straw.

Thus, the political/religious leadership of Israel begins a period of ruthless suppression of Jerusalem's Christian population; and it is Saul who executes the policy, rooting out and imprisoning the followers of Christ, with the zeal of his ambition.

Although his actions temporarily quiet the Jerusalem Christ movement, the long-term consequences will come back to haunt his bosses. He has spooked the disciples of Christ, and like cattle in a pen, they stampede. They scatter throughout Judea, taking with them the good news of Christ's Resurrection.

There is some confusion about the identity of "Philip." He could conceivably be the apostle Philip, who would later travel throughout the regions directly north and west of Judea, converting Jew and Greek alike.

Equally possible is the Greek man named Philip whom we encountered in Chapter 6 of the *Book of Acts*. This Greek Philip was made one of the seven deacons of Jerusalem, along with Stephen, when the Greeks complained that the widows among them were not getting their share of food. He was later called "Philip the Deacon" and "Philip the Evangelist," a great missionary, traveling primarily south to spread the word.

Be aware that the terms "disciple" and "apostle" are used in different ways, both in Christian dialogue and in the Bible. Either word may be used to describe one of the twelve primary followers of Jesus during His life. This became a fixed group after the Ascension, when Matthias was chosen to replace Judas as one of the "twelve."

But the term "apostle" is sometimes used to describe great disciples other than the twelve, especially those who traveled to foreign lands spreading the Gospel. In *Romans*, Paul describes himself as an "apostle of Christ."

In the Gospels, "disciple" is sometimes used to describe the twelve, but more often to describe any close follower of Jesus. In modern Christianity, people who desire to follow Christ more closely will say that they seek "discipleship."

Day 32 - The Good News is Preached in Samaria

Acts 8:9-17

Prior to that time, a man named Simon had practiced sorcery in the city and astounded the people of Samaria. He claimed to be someone great, and all the people, from the least to the greatest, heeded his words and said, "This man is the divine power called the Great Power." They paid close attention to him because he had astounded them for a long time with his sorcery.

But when they believed Philip as he preached the gospel of the kingdom of God and the name of Jesus Christ, they were baptized, both men and women. Even Simon himself believed and was baptized. He followed Philip closely and was astounded by the great signs and miracles he observed.

When the apostles in Jerusalem heard that Samaria had received the word of God, they sent Peter and John to them. On their arrival, they prayed for them to receive the Holy Spirit. For the Holy Spirit had not yet fallen upon any of them; they had simply been baptized into the name of the Lord Jesus. Then Peter and John laid their hands on them, and they received the Holy Spirit.

Commentary

Samaria is an oddity. The Samaritans were an ethno-religious nation that apparently sprung up practically in the middle of Israel, either from native Canaanites who adopted a monotheistic religion based on Judaism or by a religious schism among the Hebrews. Under the Romans, the area where the Samaritans lived was treated as a separate province, lying squarely between Judea (to the south) and Galilee (to the north).

By the time of the New Testament, the Samaritans were bitter enemies of the Israelites, often the principal enemies, as big a problem as the Philistines. This is why Christ chose a Samaritan in the famous parable of the Good Samaritan: because a Samaritan would be the last person on earth one would expect to help an injured Jew by the side of the road.

So, Samaria is really the first "Gentile" land to which the word of Christ was spread. (The Jerusalem Greeks who had converted were Greek-speaking Jews.) Remember, Christ Himself visited the borderland and converted the Samaritan woman at Jacob's well. (John 4)

We have just read that Philip went to Samaria immediately after Stephen was martyred. Simon, a witch, would probably not have been allowed to live in Judea. The conversion of such an utterly evil man, a very disciple of Satan, attests to the power of Christ and the dedication of Philip.

For some untold reason, although they are converted and baptized under Philip's influence, the Samaritan converts do not receive the Holy Spirit until Peter and John arrive.

The Sanhedrin's chasing the Christians out of Jerusalem by stoning Stephen had an unintended consequence. The disciples of Christ, being scattered by the persecution, begin to convert people not only throughout Judea, but also in another province. Like someone who throws water on burning oil, instead of quenching the flames, the Sanhedrin has only spread them wider.

Day 33 - The Sorcerer's Sin

Acts 8:18-25

When Simon saw that the Spirit was given through the laying on of the apostles' hands, he offered them money. "Give me this power as well," he said, "so that everyone on whom I lay my hands may receive the Holy Spirit."

But Peter replied, "May your silver perish with you, because you thought you could buy the gift of God with money! You have no part or share in our ministry, because your heart is not right before God. Repent, therefore, of your wickedness, and pray to the Lord. Perhaps He will forgive you for the intent of your heart. For I see that you are poisoned by bitterness and captive to iniquity."

Then Simon answered, "Pray to the Lord for me, so that nothing you have said may happen to me."

And after Peter and John had testified and spoken the word of the Lord, they returned to Jerusalem, preaching the gospel in many of the Samaritan villages.

Commentary

Simon the witch was apparently one of those who had been baptized but had not received the Holy Spirit. Like any good magician, he respects a really good trick, and (in his unholy eyes) this one is outstanding. So he tries to buy it.

Peter chastises him soundly for his wickedness, and he repents. The account of his apparent repentance ends there. Hopefully, God forgave him, but the main lesson taught in these verses does not concern Simon's specific sin, but rather, the more general issue: That the gifts of God cannot be purchased with money. Furthermore, it is evil to try to use the power of the Holy Spirit for financial gain.

We see countless attempts to purchase salvation or other favors from God with money, throughout the history of the church. And indeed, we give to the church and to the poor as an act of holiness, prescribed by God in the Bible. But at no point does the Bible tell us that our salvation is bought with our alms.

Note that Simon's name gave rise to the word "simony," a very specific sin associated with attempting to purchase or sell spiritual gifts, church offices, or sacraments.

Since everything good is a gift of God, nothing can actually be "purchased." We cannot buy; we can only rent. The legal terms of a will, or deed of land, "to _____ and his heirs forever," testifies to human vanity. We can only hold something for the duration of our lives, and even that is uncertain—anything, including land, can be taken from us or destroyed.

Nor can we designate heirs who will own something "forever." The very rich might have their names on monuments. They think it is important that their name live on, as if this has any meaning other than to extend their sinful pride past their death.

The oldest of these testimonies to human vanity, the Great Pyramid of Cheops, is well on its way to crumbling after a mere 4,500 years.

Since modern human beings have existed for 200,000 years, and the earth for 5 billion years, give or take, the Great Pyramid's existence will merely be a speck on the line of time. How much longer before the name Cheops is forgotten, and his pyramid an odd pile of rubble on a flat plain? 5,000 years? 50,000 years? 500,000 years?

Our lives are significant not because our names or works last for eternity, but because we live under the patronage of God Almighty, who existed before the world and will exist after the end of times. Our acts are significant because we can "lay up our treasure in heaven," and help others to do the same. (Matthew 6:19-21) Our lives have eternal purpose and we should use our short visit on the earth wisely.

Bonus Material: *Ozymandias*, by Percy Bysshe Shelley (1838)

I met a traveller from an antique land
Who said: Two vast and trunkless legs of stone
Stand in the desert. Near them, on the sand,
Half sunk, a shattered visage lies, whose frown,
And wrinkled lip, and sneer of cold command,
Tell that its sculptor well those passions read
Which yet survive, stamped on these lifeless things,
The hand that mocked them and the heart that fed:
And on the pedestal these words appear:

"My name is Ozymandias, King of Kings:
Look on my works, ye Mighty, and despair!"

No thing beside remains. Round the decay
Of that colossal wreck, boundless and bare
The lone and level sands stretch far away.

Day 34 - Philip and the Ethiopian Eunuch (1)

Acts 8:26-33

Now an angel of the Lord said to Philip, "Get up and go south to the desert road that goes down from Jerusalem to Gaza." So he started out, and on his way he met an Ethiopian eunuch, a court official in charge of the entire treasury of Candace, queen of the Ethiopians. He had gone to Jerusalem to worship, and on his return was sitting in his chariot reading Isaiah the prophet.

The Spirit said to Philip, "Go over to that chariot and stay by it."

So Philip ran up and heard the man reading Isaiah the prophet. "Do you understand what you are reading?" Philip asked.

"How can I," he said, "unless someone guides me?" And he invited Philip to come up and sit with him.

The eunuch was reading this passage of Scripture:

"He was led like a sheep to the slaughter,
and as a lamb before the shearer is silent,
so He did not open His mouth.
In His humiliation He was deprived of justice.
Who can recount His descendants?
For His life was removed from the earth."

Commentary

The Scriptural quote is from Isaiah 53:7, describing the suffering servant's quiet acceptance of his fate. This is a prophecy of Jesus.

After the repression brought on by the conviction and stoning of Stephen (Ch. 8), Philip fled to Samaria. Now the Holy Spirit sends him south. Gaza is a little strip of land on the Mediterranean, at the southeast corner of Judea. It was historically the stronghold of the Philistines. (In modern times, it was taken from Egypt by Israel in the War of 1967 and has been a bone of contention ever since.)

There were surely monotheists in Ethiopia at the time of today's passage, for Candace has sent the eunuch to Jerusalem to worship! He must be quite rich. He is reading from the writings of Isaiah in a Hebrew scroll, an item of high cost. Most importantly, the eunuch is studying a prophecy of Christ, so he is ripe to hear the deeper meaning of the passage from a knowledgeable teacher like Philip.

Bonus Material: Ethiopia

Ethiopia and Israel have maintained a surprising degree of connection for over 4,000 years, despite being separated by Egypt. In ancient times, the Ethiopian Empire partially absorbed two significant regions: Cush (referenced in Genesis 2:13) and Abyssinia, both situated just south of Egypt. Cush was thought to have been inhabited by the descendants of Ham, Noah's son, who went to Africa; Ham had a son named Cush. (Genesis 10:6-20)

Many Ethiopians believe that the Queen of Sheba, the Abyssinian (i.e. Ethiopian) queen who traveled to ancient Israel and had extensive interaction with King Solomon (1 Kings 10), had children by him. These children became the patriarchs and matriarchs of Ethiopia.

Others believe Ethiopia was founded by the Tribe of Dan, one of the ten lost tribes of Israel. There were certainly great migrations of Jews to Ethiopia, such as those who fled the Abyssinians during the Babylonian captivity. Haile Selassie, the last Emperor of Ethiopia (deposed in 1974), was in fact a member of what was called the "Solomonic Dynasty."

After the death of Christ, there arose a great community of Christians in Ethiopia, primarily from the active Jewish population. Despite the intrusion of Islam, Ethiopia is today 62% Christian, primarily Orthodox, although it includes various other denominations.

Day 35 - Philip and the Ethiopian Eunuch (2)

Acts 8:34-40

"Tell me," said the eunuch, "who is the prophet talking about, himself or someone else?"

Then Philip began with this very Scripture and told him the good news about Jesus.

As they traveled along the road and came to some water, the eunuch said, "Look, here is water! What is there to prevent me from being baptized?" And he gave orders to stop the chariot. Then both Philip and the eunuch went down into the water, and Philip baptized him.

When they came up out of the water, the Spirit of the Lord carried Philip away, and the eunuch saw him no more, but went on his way rejoicing. But Philip appeared at Azotus and traveled through that region, preaching the gospel in all the towns until he came to Caesarea.

Commentary

As we saw yesterday, the eunuch, an Ethiopian worshipper of Yahweh, was puzzling over Isaiah 53:7-8 when Philip encountered him:

"Like a sheep he was led to the slaughter and like a lamb before its shearer is silent, so he opens not his mouth.

In his humiliation justice was denied him. Who can describe his generation? For his life is taken away from the earth."

The eunuch was apparently reading closely and was surely interested in becoming educated about God. He was ripe to hear the Gospel, as he was studying and was curious about the most powerful prophesy in all the Bible.

One can imagine his confusion: who is Isaiah talking about? He is primed to receive the gospel of Jesus Christ — perhaps this is why the angel sent Philip to talk to him — and he is readily converted, to take the good news back to Ethiopia.

Because he was a very high official, he would have been an influential messenger to prepare Ethiopia for a more knowledgeable missionary; indeed, it was likely Philip himself who would bring the word to Ethiopia.

Remarkably, Isaiah himself predicted that a foreign Jewish eunuch would play a role in spreading the word throughout the world:

"Let not the foreigner who has joined himself to the Lord say, 'The Lord will surely separate me from his people'; and let not the eunuch say, 'Behold, I am a dry tree.'

For thus says the Lord: 'To the eunuchs who keep my Sabbaths, who choose the things that please me and hold fast my covenant,

I will give in my house and within my walls a monument and a name better than sons and daughters;

I will give them an everlasting name that shall not be cut off.'" (Isaiah 56:4-5)

The words of Isaiah seem to find specific fulfillment in Acts 8, but they might apply to anyone who does not have children of their body. The Jews, who did not practice child castration, used the word "eunuch" to apply to celibate, infertile, and/or homosexual men. Christ Himself adopts this usage in Matthew 19:12.

To remain celibate for the purpose of better serving Christ is a great blessing. Some denominations require celibacy of their leaders. There have been entire denominations whose members did not have children, so that they would not be distracted from their life of worship. The best-known of these were the American Shakers. Even more common are communities of celibacy within a denomination (such as monks).

But the most basic message is this: To know Christ and live His word is a greater good even than one of the greatest earthly gifts, creating a family. Luke, in telling the story of the Ethiopian, brings the childless special comfort so that they will not grieve. Some people, especially men, think of their children as "continuing their name"; but the Bible here lets us know that one's name is best served through service to Christ, whether or not they are blessed with children.

Acts 9 – The Conversion of Saul

Day 36 - The Conversion of Saul

Acts 9:1-9

Meanwhile, Saul was still breathing out murderous threats against the disciples of the Lord. He approached the high priest and requested letters to the synagogues in Damascus, so that if he found any men or women belonging to the Way, he could bring them as prisoners to Jerusalem.

As Saul drew near to Damascus on his journey, suddenly a light from heaven flashed around him. He fell to the ground and heard a voice say to him, "Saul, Saul, why do you persecute Me?"

[Note: Early translations, such as the KJV, added here: "*it is* hard for thee to kick against the pricks (or goads)."]

"Who are You, Lord?" Saul asked.

"I am Jesus, whom you are persecuting," He replied. "Now get up and go into the city, and you will be told what you must do."

The men traveling with Saul stood there speechless. They heard the voice but did not see anyone. Saul got up from the ground, but when he opened his eyes he could not see a thing. So they led him by the hand into Damascus. For three days he was without sight, and he did not eat or drink anything.

Commentary

Saul has "letters" — something in the nature of an arrest warrant — from the high priests. This would have included permission from the Roman authorities, because Damascus was not in Judea; it was part of the Decapolis and not under Herod's jurisdiction. His specific authority was to arrest Christians and bring them in chains to Jerusalem, where they could be tried for heresy, beaten, and imprisoned.

By all appearances, Saul is rabidly anti-Christian and eager to play henchman for the high priests.

In this famous Bible scene, Saul is knocked to the ground by a flash of light, and told by the voice of Jesus (heard by his companions) to stop persecuting Him. He is struck blind and cannot eat; but, despite this, he follows the Voice's instructions. The three-day period of suffering parallels the three days of Christ's Passion.

One phrase in older translations — "It is hard for you to kick against the goads (or pricks)" — requires explanation to understand. A goad or prick was a sharp stick used to drive cattle. In ancient Greek and Roman times, "kicking against the goads" became an idiom for opposing a deity. Like, a god would be prodding someone to do something, and the person was resisting the prod. So we infer that Saul, deep in his heart, was already troubled by his actions. He perhaps suspected that he was opposing God. (*Note*: This phrase is omitted from many translations of Acts 9, but it is well-attested in Acts 26:14.)

(*Another Note*: In Biblical exegesis, the term "well-attested" means "great scholars feel confident that it belongs in the Bible," i.e. that it was in the original manuscript.)

We must remember that Saul was not some heathen murderer. He believed in God and was a devout Jew. He had just been listening to the wrong people! Hearing the voice of God in such a miraculous manner, saying "I am Jesus," would thus have had a profound impact on him. His heart was fertile soil for the seeds of salvation; and his innovative and energetic nature, shown in his zealous pursuit of heretical Christians, will remain with him after his conversion.

Application Question:

God was willing to forgive those who murdered His Son; and now, He not only forgives Saul, one of the men who murdered Stephen, but also turns him into His greatest spokesman.

How important is it for us to overcome our urge for "justice" and revenge? How can we accomplish such a difficult task?

Day 37 - Ananias Baptizes Saul

Acts 9:10-19

In Damascus there was a disciple named Ananias. The Lord spoke to him in a vision, "Ananias!"

"Here I am, Lord," he answered.

"Get up!" the Lord told him. "Go to the house of Judas on Straight Street and ask for a man from Tarsus named Saul, for he is praying. In a vision he has seen a man named Ananias come and place his hands on him to restore his sight."

But Ananias answered, "Lord, many people have told me about this man and all the harm he has done to Your saints in Jerusalem. And now he is here with authority from the chief priests to arrest all who call on Your name."

"Go!" said the Lord. "This man is My chosen instrument to carry My name before the Gentiles and their kings, and before the people of Israel. I will show him how much he must suffer for My name."

So Ananias went to the house, and when he arrived, he placed his hands on Saul. "Brother Saul," he said, "the Lord Jesus, who appeared to you on the road as you were coming here, has sent me so that you may see again and be filled with the Holy Spirit."

At that instant, something like scales fell from Saul's eyes, and his sight was restored. He got up and was baptized, and after taking some food, he regained his strength. And he spent several days with the disciples in Damascus.

Commentary

Can you imagine what was going through Ananias' mind when the Lord told him to go find Saul of Tarsus and lay his hands on him? Saul was by this time infamous among the followers of Christ. Asking one of them to seek out Saul was like asking a German Jew in 1940 to go and find Heinrich Himmler.

But God chose Saul to spread His word to the world. It takes only the faith of one man, Ananias, to initiate this change.

God did not need Ananias to help Him change Saul. He could have sent an angel to heal Saul's blindness. He used Ananias to demonstrate a point to us — that we must be ready to follow Jesus' command to forgive our neighbor.

The clear lesson is that we must not harden our hearts to anyone. We must be prepared to forgive even the powerful and hostile. Saul was, in effect, a mass persecutor of a class of people that included Ananias. But Ananias showed us just how great our forgiveness of others must be. If they really do change, we cannot harbor either vengeance or fear of them.

Finally, these verses contain the famous words, "like scales falling from his eyes." Saul literally "saw the light." Remember John 1:4, "In him was life; and the life was the light of men." Saul's blindness and subsequent regaining of his vision is an outward manifestation of the miracle that occurs within him. "Light" is a metaphor for the Word of God. Saul is made physically blind, to demonstrate his realization that he has been blind to the light. Again in John 1:5, "the light shined in darkness, and the darkness comprehended it not."

And now the scales fall from Saul's eyes; he sees the light clearly, and undergoes an absolute transformation, from the greatest suppressor of Christianity to its greatest missionary.

Application Question:

It was terribly difficult for Ananias to reconcile with someone who had been his enemy, and we experience this same struggle. We all have people we just do not like, people who threaten or even terrify us, people we don't want to talk to.

Are we ready in our hearts to change our attitude towards them? How can we refuse to let our emotions become calcified and decide someone is our enemy (or simply someone we dislike) forever, based on past experience?

Day 38 - Saul Proclaims Jesus in Damascus

Acts 9:19-25

And after taking some food, he [Saul] regained his strength. And he spent several days with the disciples in Damascus.

Saul promptly began to proclaim Jesus in the synagogues, declaring, "He is the Son of God."

All who heard him were astounded and asked, "Isn't this the man who wreaked havoc in Jerusalem on those who call on this name? And hasn't he come here to take them as prisoners to the chief priests?"

But Saul was empowered all the more, and he confounded the Jews living in Damascus by proving that Jesus is the Christ.

After many days had passed, the Jews conspired to kill him, but Saul learned of their plot. Day and night they watched the city gates in order to kill him. One night, however, his disciples took him and lowered him in a basket through a window in the wall.

Commentary

The anti-Christian Jews who were expecting Saul's arrival are naturally upset that their policeman has sided with the criminals, to the point that he is encouraging others to join them. He has quickly become the strongest voice for Christ in the city. They are determined to kill him as he leaves Damascus; the hunter has become the hunted. But in the first of many escapes Paul makes in *Acts*, he bypasses the gates of the city by having his allies lower him over the wall in a basket.

From his description and deeds, *Acts* presents Saul/Paul as a man gifted by nature. He is a natural leader, possessing the power to persuade others, a man of enormous energy, intelligence, and resourcefulness. The Sanhedrin had made him their agent in the field in recognition of his great abilities; but now, the tide has turned. Their brilliant young champion has turned his coat, and the Christians will find him even more useful than did the Jewish leadership.

For students of the Bible, Acts 9 is one of the best-known and most important Bible stories. Many of us conceive of a Christian convert as a person who chooses Christ of his or her free will. But Paul did not choose Christ; Christ chose him. God reached down with His mighty hand and slapped Saul off his horse. Wakeup call! Paul, like a secondary version of Christ Himself, was called by God before his birth, to become the great teacher of the Gentiles.

Thus, he became a second line of communication to Christ. The first were the Apostles who knew Jesus in the flesh and continued His work after His Ascension. They were empowered and accredited first by Jesus, and then by the Holy Spirit. St. Peter might be seen as the primary figure representing the first conduit of the good news.

But in Paul's conversion, we have a second source of the Gospel: A direct contact with humanity by the ascended Christ. Paul was taught, accredited, and empowered directly by Christ <u>after</u> He had left the earth.

Day 39 - Saul (Paul) in Jerusalem

Acts 9:26-31

When Saul arrived in Jerusalem, he tried to join the disciples, but they were all afraid of him, not believing that he was a disciple. Then Barnabas brought him to the apostles and described how Saul had seen the Lord, who spoke to him on the road to Damascus, and how Saul had spoken boldly in that city in the name of Jesus.

So Saul stayed with them, moving about freely in Jerusalem and speaking boldly in the name of the Lord. He talked and debated with the Grecian Jews, but they tried to kill him. When the brothers learned of this, they took him down to Caesarea and sent him off to Tarsus.

Then the church throughout Judea, Galilee, and Samaria experienced a time of peace. It grew in strength and numbers, living in the fear of the Lord and the encouragement of the Holy Spirit.

Commentary

In reading *Acts*, we must remember the primitive conditions under which it was written. Writing such a lengthy narrative was challenging. Editing was impossible. Which is to say, we are going to see significant discontinuity and time gaps in parts of the text. Let's not wish it were ten times longer and better organized; but rather, rejoice that it exists at all. It is a miracle that we can read such a long and detailed account 2,000 years later!

Here, one would assume that Saul was lowered over a wall in Damascus and then proceeded to Jerusalem. But no. We will learn in *Galatians* that there was a huge gap of time, at least three years, before he arrived in Jerusalem. He spent most of these years in Arabia, apparently meditating and learning the Gospel from Christ. (Galatians 1:15-18)

In today's reading, we catch up with Saul in Jerusalem after his time in Arabia and Damascus. The Christians of Jerusalem fear him; they remember him as a persecutor. They might hear him preach the Gospel, but they are not convinced. Perhaps they feared Saul was creating a ruse to infiltrate their number, planning their arrest.

He is sponsored by a man named Barnabas, however, and the apostles take him in. And his actions speak louder than Barnabas' words. He preaches so avidly that he soon finds himself in the crosshairs of the anti-Christians; the apostles have to hustle him out of town. First, he goes to Caesarea, the capital of the Roman prefect (Pontius Pilate), and then to his birthplace, Tarsus, in eastern Anatolia (Turkey).

We have not really met Barnabas at this point; he will appear prominently in later chapters. Christianity, a new and growing organization, has attracted some new men of great talent and energy.

The Twelve Apostles show their humility (and intelligence) in allowing new leaders to arise; the founders do not seek to hold all the power to themselves, but freely encourage these new men to assume leadership. In Acts 6, we have already seen them make seven Greek Jews the first deacons of the church in Jerusalem; we will soon see how both Barnabas and Saul (Paul) are elevated in status.

Application Question:

We should remember the Apostles' humility and bring it into our lives. Christianity is not about gaining power and prestige within a church, a community, or a nation. Disputes over who should run things and who should have a more prestigious title are antithetical to the tenets of Christianity.

Here are some questions to ponder:

1) How can we better serve Christ, rather than our pride?
2) Do we truly believe that it is more important to preach the Gospel and to show God's Holy Spirit through following His commandments of humility and love, than to be loved and respected by other people?
3) How do we show that we expect our reward in Heaven, not on Earth?

Day 40 - Peter Heals Aeneas and Raises Dorcas

Acts 9:32-43

As Peter traveled throughout the area, he went to visit the saints in Lydda. There he found a man named Aeneas, who had been paralyzed and bedridden for eight years. "Aeneas," Peter said to him, "Jesus Christ heals you! Get up and put away your mat." Immediately Aeneas got up, and all who lived in Lydda and Sharon saw him and turned to the Lord.

In Joppa there was a disciple named Tabitha (which is translated as Dorcas), who was always occupied with works of kindness and charity. At that time, however, she became sick and died, and her body was washed and placed in an upper room. Since Lydda was near Joppa, the disciples heard that Peter was there and sent two men to urge him, "Come to us without delay."

So Peter got up and went with them. On his arrival, they took him to the upper room. All the widows stood around him, weeping and showing him the tunics and other clothing that Dorcas had made while she was still with them.

Then Peter sent them all out of the room. He knelt down and prayed, and turning toward her body, he said, "Tabitha, get up!" She opened her eyes, and seeing Peter, she sat up. Peter took her by the hand

and helped her up. Then he called the saints and widows and presented her to them alive.

This became known all over Joppa, and many people believed in the Lord. And Peter stayed for several days in Joppa with a tanner named Simon.

Commentary

Acts has left the story of Saul and returned to Peter. One of the difficulties in reading *Acts* is that it jumps from person to person and from place to place. Luckily, it is generally easy to read. Unlike much of the New Testament (such as Paul's epistles or *Revelation*), where the text is often dense and filled with subtleties and symbolism, most of *Acts* is a straightforward account of events.

During this period, called the Age of Apostles, a number of miracles were still being performed. Two of them are recounted today; Peter heals a chronically ill man and raises a woman from apparent death.

It is impossible to know God's mind. During the Apostolic Age, the apostles performed miracles similar to those performed by Christ himself. Peter, in particular, has miracles recorded. The Christians in Joppa send for him when Tabitha dies.

One of the tests of faith for the modern Christian is that today such miracles are rarely, if ever, seen. (Christians may disagree honestly about how many "miracles" occur, but I have never seen a credible instance of public resurrection.) I think most Christians accept Christ without expecting to see holy men who publicly raise people from the dead or restore chronically ill people to health.

Nobody can really say why this is. Most Christian denominations (or individuals) believe that God has not sent a prophet to explain it. Unfortunately, charlatans claiming to act in God's name will sometimes fake miracles in order to get donations. It is very discouraging, sometimes, to see hucksters making a mockery of our faith.

But miracles occur every day, and they are available for every person to see. The sun comes up in the morning. We recover from illnesses, either spontaneously or with the help of modern medicine.

Scientists scoff at these miracles, believing that they occur from "nature," but their knowledge is shallow. Take, as a small example, penicillin. A doctor might say that he has healed a person with penicillin; it is not a miracle, he could say, but the intelligence of man using a naturally occurring fungus. But who made the fungus?

He might tell you that the fungus occurred as an accident of nature, or through natural selection and evolution. He will point out that chemists have recreated the miracle molecule and improved upon it. But where did the molecules come from, and why do they work? If you continue to ask any scientist these basic questions, he will — he must — eventually say, "I don't know." An honest scientist will simply admit that he does not understand the forces that hold the universe together, much less how or why it came into existence.

Perhaps, as our knowledge increases, God expects us to see his miracles in a way appropriate to the age we live in. People who would have been "dead" two thousand years ago are still raised; people with illnesses that would have been fatal two thousand years ago are still cured. God's miracles are everywhere; we only have to see them.

Note that both the Greek name Dorcas (gazelle) and the Hebrew name Tabitha are given. While the specific story deals with Peter and Judean Christians, Luke intends that the account be read by both Jews and Gentiles.

Finally, Simon's occupation is significant. Judaism considered the tanning occupation unclean; thus, tanneries were unclean and off-limits. If Peter were following Judaism, the religion in which he was raised, he would not be allowed even to enter Simon's house, much less stay there. We will see throughout *Acts* (especially in Chapter 15) many issues and difficulties involved in reconciling Gentiles and Jews into one body, the Christian church.

Acts 10 – Peter and Cornelius

Day 41 - Peter and Cornelius (1)

Acts 10:1-8

At Caesarea there was a man named Cornelius, a centurion in what was called the Italian Regiment. He and all his household were devout and God-fearing. He gave generously to the people and prayed to God regularly. One day at about the ninth hour, he had a clear vision of an angel of God who came to him and said, "Cornelius!"

Cornelius stared at him in fear and asked, "What is it, Lord?"

The angel answered, "Your prayers and gifts to the poor have ascended as a memorial offering before God. Now send men to Joppa to call for a man named Simon who is called Peter. He is staying with Simon the tanner, whose house is by the sea."

When the angel who spoke to him had gone, Cornelius called two of his servants and a devout soldier from among his attendants. He explained what had happened and sent them to Joppa.

Commentary

Caesarea (not Jerusalem!) was the capital of Roman Judea. There were Roman troops in it to protect the officials, and Cornelius was one. A cohort (one-tenth of a legion) had about 600 men; a centurion was the head of 100 of them. (*Note*: the Latin root word "cent-" means "100," and we still see it in modern English — for example, in "century," 100 years.)

Cohorts were named for the place they were recruited, so one might expect that Cornelius would be Italian. Indeed, it would make sense that the capital would be guarded by men the prefect Pontius Pilate could trust. Being called Italian rather than Roman, they would have been from outside Rome itself, perhaps men trying to become citizens, or draftees, or simply poor men trying to make a career.

Though he is described as devout, we get several clues that Cornelius was not Jewish: First, Peter will later treat him as unclean; second, he uses a Latin name; and third, he is in the Italian Regiment. Religious belief, however, could be as odd then as now. We will encounter a number of non-Jewish monotheists in the coming chapters. Perhaps they were influenced by Jews, who were dispersed throughout the Roman Empire.

We previously learned (Day 32) that Samaria had a variant worship of YHWH, similar to Judaism, but different enough that the Jews despised the Samaritans. We also saw the Ethiopian eunuch reading Isaiah. And now we learn that a Gentile Roman soldier, Cornelius, had somehow assimilated some of the beliefs and practices of Judaism during his stay in Judea, for he is described as "devout." He gives to the poor, and prays for them.

When God's purpose is very specific, He often sends an angel to deliver a message. (In fact, *angelos* means "messenger" in Greek.) And such is the case here. An angel is sent to tell Cornelius the exact location of Peter. We might infer that Cornelius was chosen by God, for a specific purpose, because he was reverent and faithful to the God of the Jews.

The angel also informs him that God has a mission for him. We suspect this will involve the spread of the Gospel, but it will make for a colorful story in the next few lessons.

Day 42 - Peter and Cornelius (2)

Acts 10:9-16

The next day at about the sixth hour [noon], as the men were approaching the city on their journey, Peter went up on the roof to pray. He became hungry and wanted something to eat, but while the meal was being prepared, he fell into a trance.

He saw heaven open and something like a large sheet being let down to earth by its four corners. It contained all kinds of four-footed animals and reptiles of the earth, as well as birds of the air. Then a voice said to him: "Get up, Peter, kill and eat!"

"No, Lord!" Peter answered. "I have never eaten anything impure or unclean."

The voice spoke to him a second time: "Do not call anything impure that God has made clean."

This happened three times, and all at once the sheet was taken back up into heaven.

Commentary

The people referred to as "the men" in the first sentence are those sent by Cornelius, who are traveling to Joppa to see Peter. While they are en route, Peter goes up on the rooftop and has a vision, the weird sort of vision not often seen in the New Testament, outside *Revelation*.

A great sheet filled with all the animals of the earth is lowered by God himself, for Peter to eat. (This did not literally happen; *Acts* makes clear that it is a vision or dream, not an actual occurrence.) But there are problems at Peter's picnic — many of the animals of the earth are unclean and cannot be eaten by a Jew.

God is preparing Peter for the conversion of the Gentiles, specifically for the conversion of Cornelius. Just as eating certain animals is unclean to Jews, associating intimately with Gentiles is unclean. It was ingrained in Peter and had become such a strong habit that he could not overcome it. He had been raised as a good Jew; he had been taught that loving God meant not eating unclean animals or associating with unclean persons.

But God lets Peter know that things have changed. Pigs and shellfish are not forbidden to eat by nature, but by God's command; and thus, God can command that they now be clean. Just so, God can revoke his rules about associating with Gentiles, and Peter will have to learn to accept this new rule if he is to accomplish his mission.

(Note that Peter has already begun to adapt to unclean circumstances, by staying with Simon the tanner.)

The four corners of the sheet refer to the "four corners of the earth," an expression that comes from Isaiah 11:12. Peter is to bring the gospel to all people in every land on the earth. He will have to put aside his prejudices!

And so must we. Where we have commandments and instructions from the Bible, we face the difficult task of setting aside much we have learned both from secular teachers and from experience in the world; we must often set aside our habits, our desires, and our prejudices in order to accomplish God's will for our lives.

Application Question: Hearing What the Bible Actually Says

What messages from the Bible do I have the most difficulty hearing, and why are they difficult for me to hear?

We will flesh out one cause of bias in our next application question, dealing specifically with our bias to believe what we have previously heard – especially in our childhood. But there are many other biases: a Biblical teaching might disagree with our culture, or be inconvenient to follow, or be embarrassing. And we might simply be stubborn!

Day 43 - Peter and Cornelius (3)

Acts 10:17-26

While Peter was puzzling over the meaning of the vision, the men sent by Cornelius found Simon's house and approached the gate. They called out to ask if Simon called Peter was staying there.

As Peter continued to reflect on the vision, the Spirit said to him, "Behold, three men are looking for you. So get up! Go downstairs and accompany them without hesitation, because I have sent them."

So Peter went down to the men and said, "Here am I, the one you are looking for. Why have you come?"

"Cornelius the centurion has sent us," they said. "He is a righteous and God-fearing man with a good reputation among the whole Jewish nation. A holy angel instructed him to request your presence in his home so he could hear a message from you."

So Peter invited them in as his guests. And the next day he got ready and went with them, accompanied by some of the brothers from Joppa.

The following day he arrived in Caesarea, where Cornelius was expecting them and had called together his relatives and close friends. As Peter was about to enter, Cornelius met him and fell at his feet to worship him. But Peter helped him up. "Stand up," he said, "I am only a man myself."

Commentary

Peter's humility is a beacon for us all. He will not let Cornelius do obeisance to him, saying "I am only a man." He is first among Christ's disciples and the rock upon which Christ will build His church. He is the greatest and yet the most humble of Christ's followers.

Humility is a sweet thing, but difficult to find. The media blitzes us with celebrity worship; the value of celebrity, wealth, appearance, and position bombards our eyes and ears. We are taught that these are what we must strive for. Above all, recognition and adoration by crowds seem to be the most sought-after rewards.

But the value of humility is also taught. Programs for addicts and alcoholics stress humility as a foundation of sobriety. School teachers and coaches, if we are lucky, make a point of trying to instill it in the young, for pride is a great temptation for the young and talented: athletes, musicians, scholars, etc.

How can we cultivate humility in our own lives? Pray for it, of course, but even more, we must recognize pride in ourselves — something much more difficult than recognizing it in others.

One common manifestation of pride is our belief, or that of most of us, that we can run the government or some organization better than whoever is in charge. But we do not understand the difficulties. We see the splinter in someone else's eye more easily than the stick in our own.

It is hard to give the reins over to God and realize that He is running everything. He is the director and we are the actors. The weight of the world is not upon our shoulders; it would crush us. Yet the Bible teaches us, time and again, to give this burden over to God. "Trust in Him at all times, you people; pour out your hearts to Him, for God is our refuge." (Psalm 62:8)

Reinhold Niebuhr wrote a beautiful prayer about personal effort: "Give me the serenity to accept the things I cannot change, the courage to change the things that I can, and the wisdom to know the difference."

Day 44 - Peter and Cornelius (4) — Gentiles Hear the Good News

Acts 10:27-35

As Peter talked with him, he went inside and found many people gathered together. He said to them, "You know how unlawful it is for a Jew to associate with a foreigner or visit him. But God has shown me that I should not call any man impure or unclean. So when I was invited, I came without objection. I ask, then, why have you sent for me?"

Cornelius answered: "Four days ago I was in my house praying at this, the ninth hour. Suddenly a man in radiant clothing stood before me and said, 'Cornelius, your prayer has been heard, and your gifts to the poor have been remembered before God. Therefore send to Joppa for Simon, who is called Peter. He is a guest in the home of Simon the tanner, by the sea.'

So I sent for you immediately, and you were kind enough to come. Now then, we are all here in the presence of God to listen to everything the Lord has instructed you to tell us."

Then Peter began to speak: "I now truly understand that God does not show favoritism, but welcomes those from every nation who fear Him and do what is right."

Commentary

Peter comes to understand his vision with alacrity. God's demand that he eat unclean animals extended far beyond his diet. It was a command that he keep company with all sorts of people, Jew and Gentile, Judean and foreigner, in every part of the world.

Christ himself taught this lesson; He was criticized for eating with Gentiles and Samaritans. (*E.g.* Luke 5:29-39.) But for the devout Jews from which Christianity took its early members, this is a difficult lesson to accept. They were the most insular race conceivable. From the time they could speak, they were trained that to enter the house of a non-Jew, to eat a meal with him, to have anything to do with him other than some basic commercial and political dealings, was an affront to God.

People who have been strictly and consistently taught something throughout their childhood generally have terrible difficulty overcoming it. If you were told as a child that the number 13 was unlucky, you might find yourself wincing every time you see it, even though as an adult you know such superstitions are ridiculous. Think about how many of your personal characteristics come from your childhood teaching, even things you might be better off questioning.

So we must respect the early Jewish disciples as they venture into the terrifying world of Gentiles and foreigners. At this point, the word of Christ has been spread almost entirely to Jews. Philip has gone to Samaria, and some have gone to Damascus, but most of the teaching has occurred among Jews in Jewish regions of the Middle East.

Now, however, God has given Peter a direct order: the day has arrived when the word and salvation of Jesus Christ should be spread to all nations and people.

Application Question: How Can we Overcome Childhood Bias

One difficulty I have noticed in reading the Bible, both in myself and in other people, is a reluctance to unlearn an incorrect fact or interpretation we learned early in life. It might be something we learned in church.

Just this week, someone told me that "the King James Bible is the only authoritative Bible." If you think about it for just ten seconds, you will realize this cannot be true. The English language did not even exist when the Bible was written. The only authoritative New Testament is written in Greek, not King James English. Translations can be accurate or off-target, but they cannot be authoritative.

There is a wealth of hogwash taught from pulpits and Sunday schools all over the world, largely because when we learn something in our early years, it is difficult to overcome it, even in the presence of clear contradiction in God's Holy word.

As we age, we should become less set in our ways, not more, because we are expected to increase in wisdom. "Wisdom is with the aged, and understanding in length of days," says Job 12:12.

Let us take Peter's struggle to heart. If our opinion disagrees with something in the Bible, or is not literally stated in the Bible, we should be suspicious that we might have a wrong idea. And especially if it is something we adopted as "truth" in our early years.

"Trust in the Lord with all your heart, and do not lean on your own understanding." (Proverbs 3:5)

Day 45 - Peter and Cornelius (5) — The Holy Spirit Falls on the Gentiles

Acts 10:34-48

Then Peter began to speak: "I now truly understand that God does not show favoritism, but welcomes those from every nation who fear Him and do what is right. He has sent this message to the people of Israel, proclaiming the gospel of peace through Jesus Christ, who is Lord of all.

You yourselves know what has happened throughout Judea, beginning in Galilee with the baptism that John proclaimed: how God anointed Jesus of Nazareth with the Holy Spirit and with power, and how Jesus went around doing good and healing all who were oppressed by the devil, because God was with Him.

We are witnesses of all that He did, both in the land of the Jews and in Jerusalem. And although they put Him to death by hanging Him on a tree, God raised Him up on the third day and caused Him to be seen— not by all the people, but by the witnesses God had chosen beforehand, by us who ate and drank with Him after He rose from the dead. And He commanded us to preach to the people and to testify that He is the One appointed by God to judge the living and the dead. All the prophets testify about Him that everyone who believes in Him receives forgiveness of sins through His name."

While Peter was still speaking these words, the Holy Spirit fell upon all who heard his message. All the circumcised believers who had accompanied Peter were astounded that the gift of the Holy Spirit had been poured out even on the Gentiles. For they heard them speaking in tongues and exalting God.

Then Peter said, "Can anyone withhold the water to baptize these people? They have received the Holy Spirit just as we have!" So he ordered that they be baptized in the name of Jesus Christ. Then they asked him to stay for a few days.

Commentary

For the first time, a group of Gentiles receives the Holy Spirit — in fact, the passage states that the Spirit was "poured out even on the Gentiles," as if this were a great surprise. They manifest their receipt of the Spirit by praising God and speaking in tongues.

Some Christians find that understanding the Holy Spirit is more difficult than understanding God the Father or Jesus; worship of Him takes a back seat. For others, primarily those termed "Pentecostalist" or "Charismatic," the Holy Spirit is emphasized in worship and in day-to-day living. But for all Christians, the Holy Spirit is a manifestation of the one true God, promised by Jesus Christ (John 14:16), and the person (or spirit) of God who lives with us on earth.

The role of the Holy Spirit today is probably the most important immediate manifestation or person of God to humanity. He is the aspect of God who dwells within us. It is the acceptance of the Holy Spirit that brings us to believe in God and gives us faith in Christ.

The Holy Spirit inspires us in our lives. It is the Holy Spirit who brings us to read and write about Christ, who gives us the strength to bear and overcome the ordeals of life in the world, who enables us to stay strong rather than giving in to the works of evil (1 Corinthians 10:13).

If you do not understand how the Spirit lives within you, imagine that you have stolen something or committed adultery, without any chance of getting caught. You will still feel bad, even though nobody will ever learn about it. There will be a voice within you for the rest of your life, telling you that you have sinned. This is the Holy Spirit, leading you to Christ and to repentance.

Yes, some atheists have a strong conscience. It is a human trait, whose purpose is to lead us to God to seek repentance. God made us in His image; and "in His image" includes a natural capacity for morality.

But how do we handle a guilty conscience? There are three basic approaches, and here we differ greatly from the pagan or atheist: 1) Confess and find forgiveness in Christ, in which case we allow the Holy

Spirit to help us; 2) lead a life haunted by guilt; or 3) simply deny our conscience and convince ourselves that we have done nothing wrong.

We must pray to the Holy Spirit, for He will bring us the fruits of faith while we are still on earth. What "fruits"? In Galatians 5:22-23, Paul tells us that the "fruit of the Spirit is love, joy, peace, patience, kindness, goodness, faithfulness, gentleness, and self-control." This is not an exclusive list, but it's a good start!

Acts 11 – The Gentiles and Antioch

Day 46 - Peter Returns to Jerusalem (1)

Acts 11:1-10

The apostles and brothers throughout Judea soon heard that the Gentiles also had received the word of God. So when Peter went up to Jerusalem, the circumcised believers took issue with him and said, "You visited uncircumcised men and ate with them."

But Peter began and explained to them the whole sequence of events: "I was in the city of Joppa praying, and in a trance I saw a vision of something like a large sheet being let down from heaven by its four corners, and it came right down to me. I looked at it closely and saw four-footed animals of the earth, wild beasts, reptiles, and birds of the air. Then I heard a voice saying to me, 'Get up, Peter, kill and eat.'

'No, Lord,' I said, 'for nothing impure or unclean has ever entered my mouth.'

But the voice spoke from heaven a second time, 'Do not call anything impure that God has made clean.'

This happened three times, and everything was drawn back up into heaven."

Commentary

Peter has now traveled from Jerusalem (driven away by the Sanhedrin's stoning of Stephen) to Lydda, Joppa, Caesarea, and many other places, circling back to Jerusalem. This is the first significant missionary journey of an apostle, and the first to go to a foreign land.

Peter instructs the Jews of Jerusalem as he had been instructed by the Holy Spirit. The difficulties faced by the Jews in fully accepting other peoples as Christians did not end with Peter's speech. Paul will struggle enormously with the issue.

Nor was the phenomenon limited to Jews, or the Age of the Apostles. The history of Christianity is riddled with suspicion of other Christians whose language, nationality, race, language, or theology is different from ours. And "suspicion" is a polite word; war, murder, slavery, wholesale theft — the entire panoply of horrible things one person can do to another — have been committed by groups of Christians against each other, often in the name of Christ himself.

Identity politics and warfare are human nature. But, as anyone who has read the Bible knows, pridefulness is not only a sin: it is the breeding ground for a panoply of other sins. Despite every teaching to the contrary, people believe that their language is somehow the language that "true" Christians speak, or their country is specially blessed by God, etc.

We all sin and fall short of the glory of God; Christians commit adultery, blasphemy, and every other manner of sin. Identity politics is no different. The important thing is to recognize our sinful conduct, admit it, ask for forgiveness, and seek to rectify it.

Let us always remember that those who profess Christ as their savior are our brothers and sisters, no matter how different they may look, act, or speak from us. This may be the hardest of God's commandments, that we love our neighbor as ourselves. And we must keep this difficulty in mind when we read about the difficulty converted Jews had in accepting Gentiles.

Application: Christians Who Do Not Look Like Us

Every one of us has a strong natural bias to associate with people we "like" – people close to us in age, income, background, race, intelligence, politics, and so on. Is it important for us to overcome this bias? What difficulties do we face?

Day 47 - Peter Returns to Jerusalem (2)

Acts 11:11-18

"Just then three men sent to me from Caesarea stopped at the house where I was staying. The Spirit told me to accompany them without hesitation. These six brothers also went with me, and we entered the man's home. He told us how he had seen an angel standing in his house and saying, 'Send to Joppa for Simon who is called Peter. He will convey to you a message by which you and all your household will be saved.'

As I began to speak, the Holy Spirit fell upon them, just as He had fallen upon us at the beginning. Then I remembered the word of the Lord, as He used to say, 'John baptized with water, but you will be baptized with the Holy Spirit.' So if God gave them the same gift He gave us who believed in the Lord Jesus Christ, who was I to hinder the work of God?"

When they heard this, their objections were put to rest, and they glorified God, saying, "So then, God has granted even the Gentiles repentance unto life."

Commentary

Peter is speaking in this passage. He shares with other Jewish Christians his recent experience, teaching (or reminding) them that the old covenant between God and the Jews has been superseded by the new covenant of Christ.

It has been difficult for him to accept since he and all the disciples are Jewish; they have spent their entire lives practicing the law that eating with Gentiles, even entering their houses, is forbidden; now, suddenly, they must change. In human terms, this is a difficult task. Peter and his six companions are agitated. They have followed God's command, however, and traveled to see and speak to Cornelius, the Roman soldier.

Now Peter fully realizes, in the depths of his soul, the importance of the vision and command he has received. When he speaks to the Gentiles, he is awed to see that the Holy Spirit descends upon them, just as it did on the Jews. God has given the same gift to the Gentiles that he gave to His chosen people. Peter accepts with humility that they are now the equals of the Jews in the eyes of God. Gentiles can be his brothers as much as Jews; it is belief in Christ, not Judaic law, that now defines the chosen people of the earth.

The conversion of the world outside Israel has now kicked into high gear!

Day 48 - Barnabas and Saul at Antioch

Acts 11:19-26

Meanwhile those scattered by the persecution that began with Stephen traveled as far as Phoenicia, Cyprus, and Antioch, speaking the message only to Jews. But some of them, men from Cyprus and Cyrene, went to Antioch and began speaking to the Greeks as well, proclaiming the good news about the Lord Jesus. The hand of the Lord was with them, and a great number of people believed and turned to the Lord.

When news of this reached the ears of the church in Jerusalem, they sent Barnabas to Antioch. When he arrived and saw the grace of God, he rejoiced and encouraged them all to abide in the Lord with all their hearts. Barnabas was a good man, full of the Holy Spirit and faith, and a great number of people were brought to the Lord.

Then Barnabas went to Tarsus to look for Saul, and when he found him, he brought him back to Antioch. So for a full year they met together with the church and taught large numbers of people. The disciples were first called Christians at Antioch.

Commentary

The geographical focus of *Acts* now turns to Antioch, a city located in Syria at the border of Cilicia, right in the northeastern corner of the Mediterranean. Antioch was a hugely important city in that time, the largest city between Jerusalem and Rome. One might compare it to Chicago, lying between New York and Los Angeles.

Those who were not in contact with Peter and had traveled far away did not know of his interaction with Cornelius. Many of them still assumed that Jesus was the Messiah specifically to the Jews, and who can blame them? Christ was, after all, the culmination of nearly 2,000 years of Jewish prophesy and devotion, stretching back to the covenant of Abraham in the foggy dawn of history. They did not even consider trying to bring Christ's word or the Holy Spirit to Gentiles.

Nevertheless, some Jewish disciples (from Cyprus and Cyrene) had arrived at the conclusion that Gentiles were eligible for salvation in Christ. One can imagine the confusion in Antioch, with one faction trying to save Greek Gentiles and another faction treating them as unclean outsiders. So, to reinforce and encourage the evangelization of Gentiles, Barnabas travels from Jerusalem to Antioch.

The word "Christians" was first used to describe the church in Antioch. (Previously, our religion had simply been called "The Way.") The new term might well have been coined because of the need to describe the members of this new interracial religion.

It will be a long battle, as we will see, but by the time Paul writes *Galatians* he will be able to teach, "There is neither Jew nor Gentile, neither slave nor free, nor is there male and female, for you are all one in Christ Jesus." (Galatians 3:28)

Day 49 - Prediction of Famine

Acts 11:27-30

In those days some prophets came down from Jerusalem to Antioch. One of them named Agabus stood up and predicted through the Spirit that a great famine would sweep across the whole world. (This happened under Claudius.) So the disciples, each according to his ability, decided to send relief to the brothers living in Judea. This they did, sending their gifts to the elders with Barnabas and Saul.

Commentary

Agabus is very likely one of the seventy disciples mentioned in Luke 9:1-6 and was known as "Agabus the Prophet." Secular Roman histories also recorded a terrible famine in Judea during the reign of Emperor Claudius, sometime around 45 A.D., about 15 years after the death of Christ. The event was recorded in numerous Roman histories.

The chronology of *Acts* after the death of Stephen is jumbled up and a bit misleading, because the events are often compressed in time. Stephen's death occurred in 35 A.D., about two to five years after Christ died. Peter's first mission, to Gaza or Sinai, began a full year later. Saul's conversion occurred the following year (37 A.D.), and Peter's mission to Samaria, and his conversion of Cornelius, around 38 A.D.

Paul (Saul) went to Tarsus in 39 A.D. Barnabas did not travel to Antioch until 43 A.D., where he stayed for about a year. Between the two events, the infamous Roman Emperor Caligula was murdered and Claudius was reluctantly made Emperor by popular acclaim (41 A.D.); Herod Agrippa became the King of Judea around this time.

So Agabus' accurate prediction of famine was apparently made roughly one or two years before the secular record of famine in Judea.

Acts 12 – James, Peter, and Herod

Day 50 - The Martyrdom of James

Acts 12:1-5

About that time, King Herod reached out to harm some who belonged to the church. He had James, the brother of John, put to death with the sword.

And seeing that this pleased the Jews, Herod proceeded to seize Peter during the Feast of Unleavened Bread. He arrested him and put him in prison, handing him over to be guarded by four squads of four soldiers each. Herod intended to bring him out to the people after the Passover.

So Peter was kept in prison, but the church was fervently praying to God for him.

Commentary

We have a pretty good idea of when James was killed: 44 A.D. The Herod then in power in Jerusalem was neither the Herod who massacred the innocent Hebrew children (Herod the Great), nor his son (Herod Antipas), who beheaded John the Baptist and ruled during the Crucifixion. This is yet another villain named Herod: Herod Agrippa I, a grandson of Herod the Great.

Like his father and grandfather, he was a "client king" of Rome, which signifies a tad more autonomy than what we would call a "puppet"; but he ruled only with Rome's approval. There were Herods galore during this period; it is not really necessary to keep them straight, as they were all Jewish kings, clients of Rome, and viciously anti-Christian.

Herod Agrippa was as ruthless as his predecessors and did not have the religious scruples of the Sanhedrin (although he was supportive of them). If he did not like someone, he killed them. He simply ordered

James to be put to death by the sword—probably beheaded. The James here is "James the Greater," the son of Zebedee and the Apostle John's elder brother.

Background Information: Saint James

In today's Scripture, James becomes the first apostle to be martyred, and he is one of the most celebrated saints because of it.

He was reputed to have a fiery temper; Jesus called him and his brother John "the sons of Thunder." Perhaps it was this trait that got him killed so early! Other historical sources state that James traveled to Iberia (which was a major stop on Phoenician trade routes) before he returned to Jerusalem and died. He is the patron saint of both Spain and pilgrims.

An enormous body of folklore grew up around him. His body was supposedly transported to Santiago de Compostela by angels, and it is his remains in the Cathedral that make it the highly significant endpoint of the famous pilgrimage, Camino de Santiago. (Santiago, or Sant Iago, is Galician for "Saint James.")

In Spain, he is depicted with scallop shells on his hat. These are his symbol (and the symbol of the Camino); he reportedly appeared, miraculously, to save a holy knight who was drowning, but emerged from the ocean covered in scallops. The French dish of scallops in a wine sauce — "coquilles St. Jacques" — is named for this miracle.

Day 51 - God Releases Peter from Prison (1)

Acts 12:6-10

On the night before Herod was to bring him to trial, Peter was sleeping between two soldiers, bound with two chains, with sentries standing guard at the entrance to the prison. Suddenly an angel of the Lord appeared and a light shone in the cell. He tapped Peter on the side and woke him up, saying, "Get up quickly." And the chains fell off his wrists. "Get dressed and put on your sandals," said the angel. Peter did so, and the angel told him, "Wrap your cloak around you and follow me."

So Peter followed him out, but he was unaware that what the angel was doing was real. He thought he was only seeing a vision. They passed the first and second guards and came to the iron gate leading to the city, which opened for them by itself. When they had gone outside and walked the length of one block, the angel suddenly left him.

Commentary

Peter is once again rescued from prison by God. There is no earthquake this time; an angel simply strikes off his chains, has him cover himself with his cloak, walks him past the guards, and opens a gate in the city for him.

As we learned earlier, "angel" comes from the Greek word *angelos*, meaning "messenger." And indeed, we see the word *angelos* used repeatedly in the Bible to designate a non-angelic messenger. Satan's messengers are called *angeloi* (plural of *angelos*), as are the messengers sent by generals, kings, etc. So is the word angel a fabrication of English?

No, the word *angelos*, standing by itself, sometimes means "angel"! The word is used repeatedly in the first two verses of Hebrews with a very specific meaning: A real being, a creature who actually exists, serving God and living on a higher plane than human beings. (See Hebrews 2:7)

Why does God send an angel to perform a miracle for Peter, when the Holy Spirit has already been sent to him? The Bible does not tell us. We might conjecture that God does not want Peter using the Holy Spirit for his own benefit. Peter is a vessel of the Spirit, not a superhero from Marvel Comics; perhaps God does not want him to free himself from prison.

In the New Testament, we see physical prisons used repeatedly as metaphors for our physical bodies, and release from prison representing the freedom from physical limitation and death, given to us by the sacrifice of Jesus Christ. So we might again infer that, while Peter channels the Holy Spirit so powerfully that he sometimes raises the dead, he cannot save his own life: It is the power of God, not the power of Peter, which overcomes death.

Can we overcome the temptation to sin—free ourselves from the prison of our bodily desire—by our own power? Well, sometimes. Men sometimes break out of prison using their own devices. But what if we cannot overcome the temptation to sin by our own power? Will the Holy Spirit do it for us? Yes. It is a promise God has made. (1 Cor. 10:13)

Day 52- God Releases Peter from Prison (2)

Acts 12:11-19

Then Peter came to himself and said, "Now I know for sure that the Lord has sent His angel and rescued me from Herod's grasp and from everything the Jewish people were anticipating."

And when he had realized this, he went to the house of Mary the mother of John, also called Mark, where many people had gathered together and were praying. He knocked at the outer gate, and a servant girl named Rhoda came to answer it. When she recognized Peter's voice, she was so overjoyed that she forgot to open the gate, but ran inside and announced, "Peter is standing at the gate!"

"You are out of your mind," they told her. But when she kept insisting it was so, they said, "It must be his angel."

But Peter kept on knocking, and when they opened the door and saw him, they were astounded. Peter motioned with his hand for silence, and he described how the Lord had brought him out of the prison. "Send word to James and to the brothers," he said, and he left for another place.

At daybreak there was no small commotion among the soldiers as to what had become of Peter. After Herod had searched for him unsuccessfully, he examined the guards and ordered that they be executed. Then he went down from Judea to Caesarea and spent some time there.

Commentary

We find ourselves at the house of Mary, mother of John also known as Mark. Just what we needed — another woman named Mary and another man named John and/or Mark! This man (whom we will call "John Mark") is not fully identified in the Bible, but scholars have long believed that he is Mark the Evangelist.

In a nice symbolic scene, Peter knocks on the door of the house. Although the servant recognizes him, nobody believes her, and they do not want to let him in. It takes the servant—the lowliest member of the household—to convince them. The drama parallels the life and teaching of Christ in several ways, *e.g.* Luke 12:35-40.

But Peter's troubles, and those of the other believers, are growing. While the high priests of the Sanhedrin could be hypocrites and would stoop to killing heretics, they were men of God and lived (at least to some degree) under the Law of Moses. However misguided, the only murders they committed were Jesus himself and Stephen, on grounds of heresy and blasphemy. They have, however, let Peter and John go free twice, despite the disciples' teaching Christ's divinity right on a porch of the temple. And even though Stephen was stoned in a fit of temper, he was given a trial first.

Herod is another matter. Here is a truly evil man who will murder at the least provocation. He is an Eastern potentate who, unlike the Sanhedrin, has no regard for human life at all. (The Herods were not even fully Jewish, although it is a complex issue. They were the descendants of Edomites, the semi-Jewish tribe founded by Esau to the southeast of Israel.)

We must remember that his grandfather, Herod the Great, murdered scores of innocent babies simply because he feared that one of them would become "king." (Matthew 2:1-18) And his uncle, Herod Antipas, beheaded John the Baptist for no reason except that his stepdaughter danced for him. Today's passage gives us a reminder of Herodian character, by recounting Herod Agrippa I's casual murder of his guards.

The apostles and other disciples of Jesus now face a whole new level of danger. They have appeared on Herod's radar. He wants to appease the Sanhedrin, because of their political clout. Luckily, the followers of Christ are not a great danger to him personally, so he does not go on a rampage against them. If he finds them, however, he will not have qualms about killing them on the spot, with no more conscience than swatting a fly.

The increasing numbers and influence of Christ's followers create in Herod a fear of political opposition; and one cannot imagine anything more dangerous.

Day 53 - The Death of Herod Agrippa

Acts 12:20-25

Now Herod was in a furious dispute with the people of Tyre and Sidon, and they convened before him. Having secured the support of Blastus, the king's chamberlain, they asked for peace, because their region depended on the king's country for food. On the appointed day, Herod donned his royal robes, sat on his throne, and addressed the people. And they began to shout, "This is the voice of a god, not a man!"

Immediately, because Herod did not give glory to God, an angel of the Lord struck him down, and he was eaten by worms and died.

But the word of God continued to spread and multiply.

When Barnabas and Saul had fulfilled their mission to Jerusalem, they returned, bringing with them John, also called Mark.

Commentary

The third and last of the great King Herods in Judea, Herod Agrippa I, died suddenly in about 44 A.D. Although he was mostly Jewish by religion and ancestry, he was raised in Rome and was a good friend of Caligula and then Claudius. (In fact, he appears as a character in Robert Graves' famous book, *I, Claudius*.) He became more powerful than even his grandfather, Herod the Great; he was known in Rome as "Agrippa I" and his son was universally called Agrippa II, sparing us Bible readers the confusion of any more Herods.

The extent of his power was much augmented by his control of Tyre and Sidon, two wealthy Phoenician cities. To the Jews and to historians in general, Agrippa was not the worst of the Herods, despite his tendency to simply kill anyone who irritated him. He was a pro-Jewish advocate in Rome; for example, he successfully prevented Rome from desecrating the Temple of Jerusalem by erecting a statue to a Roman god.

But as a friend to the Jews—the Sanhedrin crowd—he was equally an enemy to Christians. His death by "worms" is unclear in meaning;

but other historical accounts agree that he was suddenly struck down with abdominal and chest pains, dying a few days later.

Rulers that insisted on being worshipped as gods were common before the rise of Greece, and this was revived as a practice when Rome became an empire, around the time of Christ. But God seems to take more offense when a Jew allows himself to be deified!

In the last verses, notice that the base of missionary operations has shifted to Antioch, which was in Syria, a land not dominated by the Jewish high priests and thus less hostile to the Christians. Saul and Barnabas, two of the great early missionaries, have been on a mission <u>to</u> Jerusalem — a big change from the very first missions, which went out <u>from</u> Jerusalem.

Acts 13 – Paul's First Journey

Day 54 - Barnabas and Saul on Cyprus (1)

Acts 13:1-5

Now in the church at Antioch there were prophets and teachers: Barnabas, Simeon called Niger, Lucius of Cyrene, Manaen (who had been brought up with Herod the tetrarch), and Saul. While they were worshiping the Lord and fasting, the Holy Spirit said, "Set apart for Me Barnabas and Saul for the work to which I have called them." And after they had fasted and prayed, they laid their hands on them and sent them off.

So Barnabas and Saul, sent forth by the Holy Spirit, went down to Seleucia and sailed from there to Cyprus. When they arrived at Salamis, they proclaimed the word of God in the Jewish synagogues. And John was with them as their helper.

Commentary

Up until this chapter, *Acts of the Apostles* is a history of various occurrences in the early days after Jesus' Ascension, centering somewhat on Peter, but with others being featured at different times. Beginning in Chapter 13, it refocuses entirely, onto the great teacher of Christianity, one of the most remarkable men ever to live: Paul of Tarsus. (He is still called by his Jewish name, "Saul," at this point.)

As we saw in the preceding verses, the launching pad for Christianity's spread had shifted to Antioch, an important city in Anatolia, close to the border of modern Turkey and Syria. There are several reasons for the rise of the church at Antioch. It was a large important city, it was reasonably close to Jerusalem, and it was outside the reach of the Pharisees. Perhaps most importantly, it was not in a province ruled by Herod Agrippa (such as Judea and Galilee). Agrippa was allied with the

Jewish religious authorities and had no compunctions about persecuting Christians. So the church in Antioch grew in size and prestige.

As Chapter 13 begins, the Holy Spirit has called Saul and Barnabas, two leading members of the Antioch church, on a sea journey that brought them to Barnabas' home town: the city of Salamis on the island of Cyprus. The mission was to last over two years, from 46 A.D. to 48 A.D. (See the map enclosed at the end of this book, p. 224, which delineates all of Paul's journeys described in Acts 13-28.)

We don't know for sure the identity of the "John" who went with them, but it was probably John Mark, Barnabas' cousin (see Colossians 4:10), whom most scholars also believe wrote the *Gospel of Mark*.

Day 55 - Barnabas and Saul on Cyprus (2)

Acts 13:6-12

They traveled through the whole island as far as Paphos, where they found a Jewish sorcerer and false prophet named Bar-Jesus, an attendant of the proconsul, Sergius Paulus. The proconsul, a man of intelligence, summoned Barnabas and Saul because he wanted to hear the word of God. But Elymas the sorcerer (for that is what his name means) opposed them and tried to turn the proconsul from the faith.

Then Saul, who was also called Paul, filled with the Holy Spirit, looked directly at Elymas and said, "O child of the devil and enemy of all righteousness, you are full of all kinds of deceit and trickery! Will you never stop perverting the straight ways of the Lord? Now look, the hand of the Lord is against you, and for a time you will be blind and unable to see the light of the sun." Immediately mist and darkness came over him, and he groped about, seeking someone to lead him by the hand.

When the proconsul saw what had happened, he believed, for he was astonished at the teaching about the Lord.

Commentary

Saul and Barnabas are working the island from one end to the other. It would be a difficult walk in the day; Cyprus, which is about the size of Puerto Rico, has rugged terrain. Paphos is at the opposite end from Salamis, where they started.

Although they are concentrating on synagogues, they are summoned by the "proconsul," a very senior Roman official who had previously served as a leader of the Roman Senate, far higher in rank than Pontius Pilate.

Notice that Luke now begins to call Saul "Paul." The change is permanent: in Acts 7:58-13:8 he is "Saul," a Hebrew name; and forever after he is called "Paul," which is a Greek name. We might imagine that the change is symbolic, as his ministry shifts toward conversion of the Gentiles. It might also be practical, as it would make him seem less foreign to the Greeks.

The story of the magician Bar-Jesus repeats the warning, given to us again and again in the Bible, about how witches, magicians, and superstition are regarded by God. He is the "child of the devil"—the exact opposite of Christ, the Son of God.

One of the benefits of our faith is that we may be free of these liars and fakes, who steer us away from true belief. There is no harm in enjoying a "magic" act, because it is entertainment; we are not intended to believe that the magician actually has supernatural power.

The word "magician," as used in the Bible, refers to a completely different sort of person, one who claims to exercise mystical, occult powers. The Old Testament demands that such people be put to death. Christ and his followers never put anyone to death, but they cast out demons and sometimes punished their human consorts on the spot. Here, Paul calls for Elymas to be struck blind.

Belief in something we cannot see is part of our natural makeup. Like any part of us—our sex drive, or our desire to earn money, or the strength of our arms—it can be natural and good, or it can be sinful and used to further evil, depending on how we employ it. When we are tempted to fear superstitious occurrences, we hear Satan trying to pull us away from God; when we act on our superstitions, we sin.

The number 13, a black cat, or a "ghost" have no power over us; if we give in to the fear of them, we deny the power of Christ. None of us are without sin, and we might succumb to such fears, but we still are not powerless.

We can recognize the sinfulness of superstitions and pray to be forgiven for our fears. We can fight it within ourselves and without, just as we do with all our sinful thoughts and actions. Even if we cannot rid ourselves of fear, we can remember that it crumbles against the power of the Holy Spirit, as the power of the magician Bar-Jesus crumbles before Paul and Barnabas.

Do not doubt this: Belief in Christ confers absolute immunity to superstition and "mystical" powers. The Holy Spirit will overcome them as surely as Paul blinded Elymas.

Day 56 - Paul's Sermon in "Antioch in Pisidia" (1)

Acts 13:13-25

After setting sail from Paphos, Paul and his companions came to Perga in Pamphylia, where John left them to return to Jerusalem. And from Perga, they traveled inland to Pisidian Antioch, where they entered the synagogue on the Sabbath and sat down. After the reading from the Law and the Prophets, the synagogue leaders sent word to them: "Brothers, if you have a word of encouragement for the people, please speak."

Paul stood up, motioned with his hand, and began to speak: "Men of Israel and you Gentiles who fear God, listen to me! The God of the people of Israel chose our fathers. He made them into a great people during their stay in Egypt, and with an uplifted arm He led them out of that land. He endured their conduct for about forty years in the wilderness. And having vanquished seven nations in Canaan, He gave their land to His people as an inheritance. All this took about 450 years.

After this, God gave them judges until the time of Samuel the prophet. Then the people asked for a king, and God gave them forty years under Saul son of Kish, from the tribe of Benjamin. After removing Saul, He raised up David as their king and testified about him: 'I have found David son of Jesse a man after My own heart; he will carry out My will in its entirety.'

From the descendants of this man, God has brought to Israel the Savior Jesus, as He promised. Before the arrival of Jesus, John preached a baptism of repentance to all the people of Israel. As John was completing his course, he said, 'Who do you suppose I am? I am not that One. But He is coming after me whose sandals I am not worthy to untie.'"

Commentary

We are now well into the first really long and arduous foreign journey taken by the disciples; this is commonly known as Paul's First Journey.

Paul, Barnabas, and some others come to a town named "Antioch" in central Anatolia. This town should not be confused with the great Greek city of Antioch, at the juncture of Syria and Anatolia, from which they started; so the town they reach today is called "Antioch in Pisidia," to differentiate the two.

(I am afraid that occasional difficulties with names is something the reader of *Acts* simply must accept. Double names like Bar-Jesus and "Antioch in Pisidia," uncertain and overlapping names like Mark/John/John-Mark, the same name for different places like "Asia," names for places that have changed over 2,000 years like Anatolia and Turkey – we will just have to try to keep them as straight as possible!)

Many towns in the region were named "Antioch," for this reason: After Alexander the Great died in 323 B.C., his central empire was consolidated and ruled by a king named Seleucid, whose father was the famous general Antiochus. Towns all over the Seleucid Empire were therefore named for Antiochus (at least 16 in Turkey and Syria), just as there are towns named "Jackson" or "Jacksonville" all over the United States.

One must constantly be aware of how different Syria and Turkey were 2,000 years ago, long before the area was overrun by Muslim empires (especially the Ottomans). Turkey was <u>Greek</u> in both culture and language. Syria was the remnant of Assyria. The principal tongue of Syria and Judea was Aramaic. Greek became more and more common as one moved west from Syria.

Paul was highly educated and appears to have spoken fluent Greek, as well as Aramaic and possibly Latin and/or Hebrew. (Hebrew was a long-dead language by this time, known only to Jewish scholars.) So — one more qualification for his ministry to the Gentiles!

When he begins to preach, Paul, as usual, begins with a capsule history of Judaism. Unlike Peter's great sermon in Acts 2, Paul omits Abraham and concentrates on the eras of the judges and kings. From there, he segues into the story of John the Baptist. While Paul does not mention Moses by name, he refers to him, as all the conversion sermons given to Jewish audiences do.

Paul's sermon follows a logical and rhetorically effective line; he gives the history of leadership of the Hebrews, concentrating on how God has changed the nature of the leadership: prophets, to judges, to kings, to John the Baptist. He thus prepares his audience for the idea that radical change in governance of Judaism has sound historical precedent.

Historical precedent was enormously important to the Jews; by showing that Christ's ascendancy is another step in the normal progression of Judaism, he eases his audience into the idea that Christ's teachings are part of Hebrew history. (*Cf.* Matthew 1:1-17.) That is, by teaching that Christ was the Messiah (and eventually, that He was literally the Son of God), Paul is not committing heresy. Rather, God had always intended that Christ would be the goal and the terminal point of Judaism, using the Hebrews and transforming their religion into an effective means of eternal salvation.

For similar reasons, Paul cites the prophecy of Christ's coming; and then recites John the Baptist's testimony that Jesus is this Christ. By following these steps, he ties Christ to beliefs already solidly integrated into Jewish theology. He does not preach a new religion; rather, he preaches the next step in Judaism, a step already predicted by the prophets.

Day 57- Paul's Sermon in "Antioch in Pisidia" (2)

Acts 13:26-35

"Brothers, children of Abraham, and you Gentiles who fear God, it is to us that this message of salvation has been sent. The people of Jerusalem and their rulers did not recognize Jesus, yet in condemning Him they fulfilled the words of the prophets that are read every Sabbath. And though they found no ground for a death sentence, they asked Pilate to have Him executed.

When they had carried out all that was written about Him, they took Him down from the tree and laid Him in a tomb. But God raised Him from the dead, and for many days He was seen by those who had accompanied Him from Galilee to Jerusalem. They are now His witnesses to our people.

And now we proclaim to you the good news: What God promised our fathers He has fulfilled for us, their children, by raising up Jesus. As it is written in the second Psalm:

'You are My Son;

today I have become Your Father.'

In fact, God raised Him from the dead, never to see decay. As He has said:

'I will give you the holy and sure blessings promised to David.'

So also, He says in another Psalm:

'You will not let Your Holy One see decay.'"

[Psalm 2:7; Isaiah 55:3; Psalm 16:10]

Commentary

Here, Paul continues the sermon in Antioch in Pisidia, a small town in the Roman province of Galatia (today in central Turkey). We will want to remember "Galatia" because Paul will later write an important letter to the churches there, the *Epistle to the Galatians*.)

Paul and his companions were asked by the congregation of a synagogue to speak "if they had a message of encouragement." As we come to know Paul, it should not surprise us that he accepted the invitation.

Paul was obviously an extraordinary man, one marked for leadership. When we first met him, prior to his conversion, he had become a trusted lieutenant of the Sanhedrin of Jerusalem. He was present with them at the trial of Stephen and thereafter became their trusted field agent, responsible for rounding up Christians and returning them to Jerusalem in chains.

Since the time of his conversion, he has constantly risen to the forefront of any group in which he finds himself. Note that, when this mission began, it was a mission of "Barnabas and Saul." But in Acts 13, the text has begun to refer to the group as "Paul and his companions." And when the group is asked if it wants to speak, it is Paul who stands up.

Paul was forceful, determined, and driven even before his conversion. His family shows signs of ambition; although they were tent-makers, they were Roman citizens, a rarity among Hebrews. This citizenship bespeaks a concerted effort by an ambitious forebear. Most likely, one of his recent forefathers had distinguished himself in Roman military service.

His drive to distinguish himself, and the talents which made it possible, have now been subsumed in another kind of ambition — the ambition for the glory of God. Paul will seem to struggle with humility from time to time, as we see in his many epistles, and understandably so; his name is known and revered even today.

Which of us has not struggled for humility, with considerably less cause? We are all given gifts of the Holy Spirit, and his gift was one of leadership so forceful that he became famous. So if he seems a bit proud on occasion, we must remember that he pushed himself to the forefront, not to glorify himself, but to serve God as he was called to do.

Day 58 - Paul's Sermon in "Antioch in Pisidia" (3)

Acts 13:36-43

"For when David had served God's purpose in his own generation, he fell asleep. His body was buried with his fathers and saw decay. But the One whom God raised from the dead did not see decay.

Therefore let it be known to you, brothers, that through Jesus the forgiveness of sins is proclaimed to you. Through Him everyone who believes is justified from everything you could not be justified from by the law of Moses. Watch out, then, that what was spoken by the prophets does not happen to you:

'Look, you scoffers,

wonder and perish!

For I am doing a work in your days

that you would never believe,

even if someone told you.'" *[Habakkuk 1:5]*

As Paul and Barnabas were leaving the synagogue, the people urged them to continue this message on the next Sabbath. After the synagogue was dismissed, many of the Jews and devout converts to Judaism followed Paul and Barnabas, who spoke to them and urged them to continue in the grace of God."

Commentary

Paul continues to speak in the synagogue of Antioch in Pisidia. He began in our passage yesterday with a history of the Hebrews; today, he gets to the meat of his message. He starts by showing a critical difference between King David (who was much revered) and Jesus.

David, when he had served God's purpose, died, and his body returned to the Earth to decay. But now Christ has come and defeated death. His body did not decay but returned to life and walked the Earth, for a period, before he was gathered up to heaven.

We don't often think about what happened to Christ's body, but the Bible is clear that He was resurrected physically. Remember, when people went to His tomb, it was empty; God did not simply give Christ's spirit life after death, but showed in His great power that He had created Christ's body, and He could give it life as He willed. Christ even offered to let Thomas put his fingers into His wounds. (John 20:24-29)

Now, God has begun to do the same thing for humanity that He did for Christ: give them life after death. The body of the world's population has begun to receive the promise of eternal life; and it is spreading, as Christ spread it during his lifetime on earth, through spoken transmission of the word.

As Christ Himself traveled through Judea in the few years of His ministry on earth, Paul has now begun to travel in ever-widening circles throughout the world. He witnessed to all (and continues to witness today through his writing) that it is not God, but sin, which has declared death; and that through Christ's sacrifice and grace, the sin which we have accepted can be forgiven, so that we might not die, just as Christ did not die.

Day 59 - Paul's Second Sabbath in Antioch in Pisidia

Acts 13:44-52

On the following Sabbath, nearly the whole city gathered to hear the word of the Lord. But when the Jews saw the crowds, they were filled with jealousy, and they blasphemously contradicted what Paul was saying.

Then Paul and Barnabas answered them boldly: "It was necessary to speak the word of God to you first. But since you reject it and do not consider yourselves worthy of eternal life, we now turn to the Gentiles. For this is what the Lord has commanded us:

'I have made you a light for the Gentiles,

to bring salvation to the ends of the earth.'" *[Isaiah 49:6]*

When the Gentiles heard this, they rejoiced and glorified the word of the Lord, and all who were appointed for eternal life believed. And the word of the Lord spread throughout that region.

The Jews, however, incited the religious women of prominence and the leading men of the city. They stirred up persecution against Paul and Barnabas and drove them out of their district. So they shook the dust off their feet in protest against them and went to Iconium. And the disciples were filled with joy and with the Holy Spirit.

Commentary

Paul's second sermon in the town synagogue did not go as smoothly as the first, even though the entire town turned out to hear him. The Jewish leaders were outraged by both the message Paul delivered and by the size of the crowd he drew. He was replacing them as the leading religious authority.

Unfortunately, this phenomenon has never disappeared. Religious leaders are only human, and pride in their position is a constant temptation. It applies as much to Christians as anyone else, today and throughout history. Increasing the size of one's congregation, or getting a higher-ranking office, sometimes seems to be motivated as much by personal pride as by joy at spreading the word of Christ. Priests and ministers want to become bishops and there is considerable politicking involved; pastors want to see their church congregation grow; televangelists want higher rankings and increased donations.

Human nature has not changed. The Greeks and Jews of first-century Anatolia were no more and no less susceptible to pride (not to mention lust, anger, etc.) than we are.

Note that Paul and Barnabas have fully absorbed the lesson learned by Peter in Acts 10. Whether they knew about Peter's experience with Cornelius is speculative, but they had fully accepted the need to include the Gentiles in the message of salvation. But including the Gentiles did not diminish the opposition to Christianity in the long term. Just the opposite; as we will soon see, it simply inflamed Gentile leaders (both religious and commercial) without pacifying Jewish opposition.

In addition, it would give the Jewish opposition another tool to drive a wedge between Judaism and Christianity, because many Jews will be shocked that Paul and Barnabas would even consort with unclean Gentile populations.

And thus they depart Antioch in Pisidium. You might recognize the idiom "shake the dust off their feet" from Matthew 10:14, where Jesus instructed His disciples: "If anyone will not welcome you or listen to your words, leave that home or town and shake the dust off your feet."

Put simply, if these people have heard and rejected the gospel, it is no longer Paul's problem.

Acts 14 – First Journey Cont'd

Day 60 - Paul and Barnabas in Iconium

Acts 14:1-7

At Iconium, Paul and Barnabas went as usual into the Jewish synagogue, where they spoke so well that a great number of Jews and Greeks believed. But the unbelieving Jews stirred up the Gentiles and poisoned their minds against the brothers. So Paul and Barnabas spent considerable time there, speaking boldly for the Lord, who affirmed the message of His grace by enabling them to perform signs and wonders.

The people of the city were divided. Some sided with the Jews, and others with the apostles. But when the Gentiles and Jews, together with their rulers, set out to mistreat and stone them, they found out about it and fled to the Lycaonian cities of Lystra and Derbe and to the surrounding region, where they continued to preach the gospel.

Commentary

Lycaonia was not a province, but the name of a mountainous region, like "the Ozarks." It was part of the Roman province of Galatia.

For the first time, the word "Jews" is used to classify Hebrews who do not believe in Christ; as we saw before, the followers of Christ have begun to be called Christians. So finally, in about 49 A.D., we begin to see a full separation of the two religions. Peter has accepted Gentile converts (Acts 10-11), and in Acts 15 we will see him instruct Christian Jews to accept Gentile Christians fully, as their brothers.

Christianity had been considered a splinter sect of Judaism. But the separation of the two is growing wider, and will continue to widen until they are considered different religions altogether.

The Scripture is mostly self-explanatory. Lycaonia is a backwater tribal area in south-central Anatolia, and Iconium its largest city — perhaps only a town. Really, its biggest claim to fame is that it became a well-organized Christian stronghold, due to Paul's early efforts.

Just as in Antioch in Pisidia, Paul and Barnabas have converted part of the city, and the Jewish leadership reacts violently. The apostles once again "shake the dust off their feet" and remove themselves to another area, to cause some more trouble down the road.

Day 61 - Idolatry at Lystra

Acts 14:8-13

In Lystra there sat a man crippled in his feet, who was lame from birth and had never walked. This man was listening to the words of Paul, who looked intently at him and saw that he had faith to be healed. In a loud voice Paul called out, "Stand up on your feet!" And the man jumped up and began to walk.

When the crowds saw what Paul had done, they lifted up their voices in the Lycaonian language: "The gods have come down to us in human form!" Barnabas they called Zeus, and Paul they called Hermes, because he was the chief speaker. The priest of Zeus, whose temple was just outside the city, brought bulls and wreaths to the city gates, hoping to offer a sacrifice along with the crowds.

Commentary

Don't you wish you could have seen this? It must have been hilarious. Paul has just healed a man in the name of Christ as a testimony to Christ's divinity, to bring people to the one true God, and instead, they begin yelling and screaming that the disciples are pagan gods come to earth. You can just imagine Paul and Barnabas sputtering and trying to yell over the crowd: "Stop it! We are not gods! There is only one God!!"

And the funniest part is that they start calling Barnabas "Zeus," and Paul, "Hermes." Don't you have to wonder if Paul was the tiniest bit miffed? Not only was he called a pagan god, but the god chosen for him was Barnabas' underling!

The incident illustrates how important it is for us to testify and give witness to our belief in God: Father, Son, and Holy Spirit. Things are going to happen in life that people do not understand and they will invent something to explain them. In fact, people invent supernatural entities or rituals for even normal phenomena, such as rain or removing warts.

If they do not know the truth about God and Christ, they are going to substitute a false god or gods. Although sin is in our nature, it is also in our nature to seek God. We do not need evidence of His existence; we grow towards Him like a buried tulip grows towards the sun in the spring.

The tulip analogy brings to mind Christ's parable of the seed that was sown in rocks, and in tares, and on fertile soil (Matthew 13:19-23). If people do not know the truth, then the seed of their faith can fall anywhere; often a person's most important beliefs are practically accidental. Anyone who has read the Bible, and accepted Christ, should be ready at least to let others know where the fertile soil can be found.

This parable applies also to science, where many atheists seek wisdom, but it is thorny ground for spiritual understanding; as useful and wonderful as "science" is, it is a dead-end for those who seek to know God, for it often seems to choke out the truth of the gospel.

Day 62 - Paul and Barnabas in Lystra

Acts 14:14-18

But when the apostles Barnabas and Paul found out about this, they tore their clothes and rushed into the crowd, shouting, "Men, why are you doing this? We too are only men, human like you. We are bringing you good news that you should turn from these worthless things to the living God, who made heaven and earth and sea and everything in them. In past generations, He let all nations go their own way. Yet He has not left Himself without testimony to His goodness: He gives you rain from heaven and fruitful seasons, filling your hearts with food and gladness."

Even with these words, Paul and Barnabas could hardly stop the crowds from sacrificing to them.

Commentary

Paul and Barnabas are dismayed. They have traveled all the way to Lystra to bring the people to Christ; instead, they have deepened their belief in pagan gods! They frantically tell the people that these false gods are vanity; Paul and Barnabas bring news of the true God, of Christ, and of salvation. And even though they have performed a miracle, to bolster the truth they tell, the people are "scarcely restrained" from sacrificing to them.

Human nature has not changed in 2,000 years. People become accustomed to one way of thinking and find it nearly impossible to change. We all harbor attitudes that are false and "truths" that are untrue. It is pride. Sinful pride tells us that the thoughts in our head are correct. We are stubborn, from the smallest thing to the largest.

I remember, from some years back, a huge controversy erupting in Dear Abby. Half the people thought toilet paper should be hung so that the loose end hung over the top; the other half, that toilet paper should be hung with the loose end against the wall. The debate was fierce! I don't think anyone was convinced; everyone was sure that their opinion was, somehow, objectively true.

I call this "pride of opinion." We think we know something. Perhaps we learned it in our youth. Perhaps we just heard it from a friend or even a stranger. Perhaps we even did some research or thought it over.

But however we come to our opinion, we believe it is absolutely true and <u>we cease inquiry</u>. We adopt it as part of ourselves. And if we hear something different, we interpret it as an attack on ourselves! We might make up facts and arguments to defend our opinion, even if it is proven wrong.

In *Gulliver's Travels,* by the great satirist Jonathan Swift, Gulliver travels to a land where there is a terrible war. One side believes that a boiled egg should be cracked and eaten from the large end. Their enemies, that the egg should be put in the egg cup fat side down and eaten from the narrow end.

Everyone in the world seems to know exactly how other people should drive. Neighbors harbor deep grudges about such things as the strip of grass between their driveways. Christians have shed blood over whether the sign of the cross should be made left to right (Catholic), or right to left (old Orthodox), or not at all (Protestant).

There is only one core belief that is absolutely and inflexibly true: the Word of God—the knowledge that God, through Christ, has given us the grace to be forgiven of our sins. We cannot "speak against the Holy Spirit." (Matthew 12:32)

Most everything else we hear, see, or experience in life that might contradict what we think, no matter how absolutely it contradicts our personal opinions, we must be open to. If somebody interprets the Bible differently than we do, we should listen. We do not have to accept it, but we should consider it. Otherwise, our thoughts and opinions will become controlled by pride.

I once heard an African-American man, 105 years old, on the Today Show. When asked the secret of his long life, he said: "a smart person will learn; a foolish person will stop learning." We should not go through life thinking we know everything. And what if a new roommate or spouse wants to hang the toilet paper differently from us, or our neighbor wants to put wood chips instead of grass between our driveways? Just do it. "If your neighbor sues you for your coat, give him your cloak also." (Matthew 5:40)

Day 63 - Paul Stoned at Lystra

Acts 14:19-23

Then some Jews arrived from Antioch and Iconium and won over the crowds. They stoned Paul and dragged him outside the city, presuming he was dead. But after the disciples had gathered around him, he got up and went back into the city. And the next day he left with Barnabas for Derbe.

They preached the gospel to that city and made many disciples. Then they returned to Lystra, Iconium, and Antioch, strengthening the souls of the disciples and encouraging them to continue in the faith. "We must endure many hardships to enter the kingdom of God," they said.

Paul and Barnabas appointed elders for them in each church, praying and fasting as they entrusted them to the Lord, in whom they had believed.

Commentary

Paul and Barnabas' mission to Lystra was tumultuous. Having been chased out of Iconium (in the preceding verses), 30 miles to the north, they came to Lystra. When Paul healed a man, the city hailed them as incarnations of Zeus and Hermes.

But the enemies they had made in Iconium and Antioch (in Pisidia) followed them to Lystra like a gang of thugs; and, apparently, when the people of Lystra understood that Barnabas and Paul were not, in fact, Greek gods come to earth, many of them joined the mob from the north and attacked them, stoning Paul and leaving him for dead.

Paul's dedication is tested many times in *Acts*, but none more than this. He is stoned to the point of death. I have seen a person this badly beaten, and let me tell you, the aftermath is agonizing and debilitating.

But Paul—and, one must think, with the intervention of the Holy Spirit—just gets up and keeps going. He is one tough cookie!

The two apostles (as Paul and Barnabas came to be called) and their companions were dauntless. Strengthened by the Holy Spirit, they made converts in the nearby town of Derbe and then returned to the other towns — where they had enemies who had already tried to kill them — to strengthen and organize the new devotees into more structured churches.

In each place, they appointed "elders," members of the church who were stable, respected, and devout. This is one of several leadership positions mentioned in the New Testament, in connection with the early churches; nowhere does the Bible give us a specific blueprint for how a church must be organized, but clearly, some sort of leadership is required for any group of size to function.

Bonus Discussion: Elders

The variety of terms used in the New Testament for those who lead churches (both as to practical leadership and spiritual leadership) are myriad, and their meaning often uncertain. Moreover, different translations use different English words. The Greek word used in Acts 14:23 is *presbuteros*. It comes from *presbus*, "old man," and literally means "older man"; so "elder" is a good translation for it. Today, both "elder" and/or "presbyter" are used in various denominations to denote some sort of duty or rank in church organization, usually in a local church, just as in today's lesson.

Day 64 - Paul and Barnabas Return to Antioch

Acts 14:24-28

After passing through Pisidia, they came to Pamphylia. And when they had spoken the word in Perga, they went down to Attalia.

From Attalia they sailed to Antioch, where they had been commended to the grace of God for the work they had just completed. When they arrived, they gathered the church together and reported all that God had done through them, and how He had opened the door of faith to the Gentiles. And they spent a long time there with the disciples.

Commentary

Here ends the "First Missionary Journey of Paul." He and his companions started in Antioch, sailed to Cyprus, and traveled across its length to Salamis. They then took a boat to the mainland, landing in Perga, then went north to the province of Galatia.

Once they reached Antioch in Pisidia, they traveled south through Iconia, Lystra, and Derbe, the places where they had a great deal of trouble, with an angry mob pursuing them and stoning Paul (nearly to death) at one point.

They converted numerous people in each town, founded churches, and appointed elders to oversee the churches

On the return journey, they retraced their steps south through Anatolia (Turkey) and then recrossed the sea to Antioch. The journey took somewhere between 9 and 18 months. Travel in that day was exceedingly difficult.

Needless to say, they were exhausted and happy to be back in the comparative safety and comfort of the large church in Antioch. And they report the startling news of the full inclusion of many Gentile Christians among the Christian Jews.

All the events in Acts 13 and 14 occurred in a comparatively unimportant part of the world, primarily the pastoral area called Lycaonia. The effectiveness of their efforts was considerable, for the ecclesiastical system Lycaonia was more completely organized in the 4th century than that of any other region of Asia Minor.

One might, in retrospect, view this journey as a warm-up. Because as we will soon see, on his future journeys, Paul will take on the greatest cities in the Western world.

Spoiler alert: The last verse of *Acts* finds Paul preaching in Rome itself.

Acts 15 – The Council of Jerusalem; Paul's Second Journey

Day 65 - The Jerusalem Council (1)

Acts 15:1-11

Then some men came down from Judea and were teaching the brothers, "Unless you are circumcised according to the custom of Moses, you cannot be saved." And after engaging these men in sharp debate, Paul and Barnabas were appointed, along with some other believers, to go up to Jerusalem to see the apostles and elders about this question.

Sent on their way by the church, they passed through Phoenicia and Samaria, recounting the conversion of the Gentiles and bringing great joy to all the brothers. On their arrival in Jerusalem, they were welcomed by the church and apostles and elders, to whom they reported all that God had done through them.

But some believers from the party of the Pharisees stood up and declared, "The Gentiles must be circumcised and required to obey the law of Moses." So the apostles and elders met to look into this matter.

After much discussion, Peter got up and said to them, "Brothers, you know that in the early days God made a choice among you that the Gentiles would hear from my lips the message of the gospel and believe. And God, who knows the heart, showed His approval by giving the Holy Spirit to them, just as He did to us. He made no distinction between us and them, for He cleansed their hearts by faith.

Now then, why do you test God by placing on the necks of the disciples a yoke that neither we nor our fathers have been able to bear? On the contrary, we believe it is through the grace of the Lord Jesus that we are saved, just as they are."

Commentary

Circumcision again! And this is not the last of it; the Bible will need an entire long book, the *Epistle to the Hebrews*, to finally put the matter to rest.

The controversy seems trivial and slightly unsavory to us today. It may even seem a bit out of place to be talking about such a matter in the Bible. But it was hugely important to the Jews, and remains so today, because God <u>required</u> the Jews to circumcise male children as part of the Old Covenant.

God said to Abraham, "As for you, you shall keep my covenant . . . . Every male among you shall be circumcised. . . . Any uncircumcised male who is not circumcised in the flesh of his foreskin shall be cut off from his people; he has broken my covenant." (Genesis 17:9-14)

It had been ingrained in their hearts for 2,000 years. Not to be circumcised meant that a man and his family were cut off from God. One could not have a relationship with God unless he or his parents—or for a woman, her father and/or husband—had followed the commandment. And, in early times, being cut off from one's people could result in exile and possible starvation.

Thus, although they were able to receive the word of Christ, the Jews found it very hard to understand that uncircumcised men—that is, Gentiles—were able to be in a covenant with God.

It is easy for us to accept this today. To most of us, circumcision is a minor medical decision for parents, something not discussed in polite company. But we must realize, that many of us might not be Christians today except for the work of Paul and Barnabas 2,000 years ago. Peter himself refused to preach to the Gentiles until God sent him a vision (Acts 10).

Day 66 - The Jerusalem Council (2)

Acts 15:12-21

The whole assembly fell silent as they listened to Barnabas and Paul describing the signs and wonders God had done among the Gentiles through them. When they had finished speaking, James declared,

"Brothers, listen to me! Simon has told us how God first visited the Gentiles to take from them a people to be His own. The words of the prophets agree with this, as it is written:

> 'After this I will return and rebuild
> the fallen tent of David.
> Its ruins I will rebuild,
> and I will restore it,
> so that the remnant of men may seek the Lord,
> and all the Gentiles who are called by My name,
> says the Lord who does these things
> that have been known for ages.' *[Amos 9:11-12]*

It is my judgment, therefore, that we should not cause trouble for the Gentiles who are turning to God. Instead, we should write and tell them to abstain from food polluted by idols, from sexual immorality, from the meat of strangled animals, and from blood. For Moses has been proclaimed in every city from ancient times and is read in the synagogues on every Sabbath."

Commentary

We have seen how understandably difficult it was for the Jews to accept uncircumcised Gentiles as Christians. But Barnabas and Paul are very persuasive.

The James who announces the judgment of the Council is "James the Just," the leader of the Jerusalem church and the first Bishop of Jerusalem. He was a man renowned for his piety and goodness. Many scholars believe that James the Just was the same man as the apostle called James (the Lesser). Most Protestants believe he was Jesus' half-brother; Catholics teach that he was Jesus' cousin or step-brother.

But for certain, he was pre-eminent, for he (and not Peter or John) announces the ruling of the Christian Church. James accepts the converted Gentiles, but requires them to follow certain Jewish rules of conduct, such as abstaining from sexual immorality, "what has been strangled," etc. Although the first of these sounds reasonable enough today, the second is puzzling. To understand it fully, we must consider the major issue that underlies it: Where does modern Christian morality come from?

We take for granted certain moral precepts, but we should not. Consider murder. Other than the Jews, the concept that human life is sacred in and of itself, and that murder is therefore immoral, was practically unknown 2,000 years ago. Most societies made it illegal to kill some people under some circumstances. In Rome, for example, one might be arrested and executed for killing a Roman citizen, but not a slave. And the same with theft, adultery, etc. Some people might be protected by law, but there was no sense that these actions were inherently "wrong," in and of themselves.

A general moral code that applied to all humanity simply did not exist. Some Greek philosophers speculated about inherent morality, but their influence was limited and largely theoretical.

Christ Himself was not primarily a moral teacher. Although He did give us several moral precepts, His principal message was one of forgiveness and salvation. The fundamental morality we follow comes from Judaism and the Old Testament, and Christ's limited teachings on morality were modifications of Jewish law, or examples of how impossible it was to follow the Law, rather than a full moral code.

The early Jewish Christians struggled with which of the laws they lived under were universal and which were superseded by Christ. Ultimately, church leaders would come to lean upon the Ten Commandments as the basic moral law and discard much of the rest of the Mosaic Law, but this took time.

So, we cannot judge the ancients from our armchairs in the 21st century. The Jews of 50 A.D. — perhaps the only "moral" people in the world — were understandably horrified by the eating of bloody meat, for as far as they could tell, their God had forbidden it. "For Moses has been proclaimed in every city from ancient times and is read in the synagogues on every Sabbath."

Our morals today are fundamentally Jewish. Both Christ and Paul clarified and added to the "Christian" moral code, but the concept of this moral code was foreign to Gentile converts. And so James, who had to act quickly, picked out those practices of the Gentiles which were widespread and most shocking to the Jews of Jerusalem.

Note the immense importance of sexual morality. The Greeks were notorious for their homosexuality and pederasty. One speaker in Plato's *Symposium* actually argued that sexual relations of a grown man with a male youth was "heavenly" – the highest good of sexual behavior. The current arguments about homosexuality and Christianity are not a modern phenomenon; they are identical to the issues decided by the Council of Jerusalem in 49 A.D.

Day 67 - The Council's Letter to Gentile Believers

Acts 15:22-29

Then the apostles and elders, with the whole church, decided to select men from among them to send to Antioch with Paul and Barnabas. They chose Judas called Barsabbas and Silas, two leaders among the brothers, and sent them with this letter:

"The apostles and the elders, your brothers,

To the brothers among the Gentiles in Antioch, Syria, and Cilicia:

Greetings.

It has come to our attention that some went out from us without our authorization and unsettled you, troubling your minds by what they said. So we all agreed to choose men to send to you along with our beloved Barnabas and Paul, men who have risked their lives for the name of our Lord Jesus Christ. Therefore we are sending Judas and Silas to tell you in person the same things we are writing.

It seemed good to the Holy Spirit and to us not to burden you with anything beyond these essential requirements: You must abstain from food sacrificed to idols, from blood, from the meat of strangled animals, and from sexual immorality. You will do well to avoid these things.

Farewell."

Commentary

The practices forbidden here have an oddity: Two of them — eating the meat of strangled animals, and eating blood — are acts that modern Christians generally would not equate with sin. Few of us would have any idea if we were eating meat from an animal that had been strangled. We might consider it inhumane and even protest it, if we knew about it, but we would not equate it with a literal Biblical sin. Nor do most people even remark upon blood in their meat.

But Kosher dietary laws have strict requirements. Animals must be killed humanely, and the meat must be thoroughly drained of blood and soaked in water.

And there is another curiosity about the prohibition on consuming blood: it was first given to Noah! It actually predates the Law of Moses and the birth of Abraham. When the ark landed and Noah had built an altar, and sacrificed to YHWH, God gave humanity the right to eat meat. "Every moving thing that lives shall be food for you." (Genesis 9:3) As part of this permission, however, God specified: "But you shall not eat flesh with its life, *that is,* its blood." (Genesis 9:4) This law was so ancient, so firmly established, that James and the Council of Jerusalem believed it had survived the Ascension of Christ.

As for "abstaining from sexual immorality" — I wish I could say that Christians understand the sinfulness of sexual immorality. Too often churches and church leaders openly countenance, or at least wink at, some forms of sexual misbehavior. Sexual relations other than between a married man and woman are forbidden by God, and church leaders who do not state this clearly are doing their flock a disservice.

The sexual norms of contemporary society are quite different, but (as we discussed previously) so were the sexual norms of non-Jewish culture 2,000 years ago. The Bible tells us to take our values from the word of God, not from the society we happen to live in. "Do not be conformed to the world [or the age] . . . ." (Romans 12:2)

Concerning "food sacrificed to idols," most Christians would feel discomfort at watching a heathen ritual where an animal is sacrificed to an idol. We will learn later on in the Bible that simply eating the meat sacrificed to an idol might be all right, if it does not disturb a fellow Christian. (See 1 Corinthians 8:1–6.) But the Council perhaps wanted new Gentile Christians to stay away from questionable conduct; or perhaps thought the faith of new Gentile converts was too young to fully ignore a sacrifice that a more mature Christian would simply find meaningless. (Again, see 1 Corinthians 8.)

Finally, note that Paul apparently undermined all commandments concerning what a Christian can eat, in Colossians 2.

Day 68 - Paul Begins His Second Journey

Acts 15:30-41

So the men were sent off and went down to Antioch, where they assembled the congregation and delivered the letter. When the people read it, they rejoiced at its encouraging message.

Judas and Silas, who themselves were prophets, said much to encourage and strengthen the brothers. After spending some time there, they were sent off by the brothers in peace to return to those who had sent them. But Paul and Barnabas remained at Antioch, along with many others, teaching and preaching the word of the Lord.

Some time later Paul said to Barnabas, "Let us go back and visit the brothers in every town where we proclaimed the word of the Lord, to see how they are doing." Barnabas wanted to take John, also called Mark. But Paul thought it best not to take him, because he had deserted them in Pamphylia and had not accompanied them in the work.

Their disagreement was so sharp that they parted company. Barnabas took Mark and sailed for Cyprus, but Paul chose Silas and left, commended by the brothers to the grace of the Lord. And he traveled through Syria and Cilicia, strengthening the churches.

Commentary

The four men mentioned in the first sentence are Paul, Barnabas, and two leaders from the church of Jerusalem: Silas and Judas (Barsabbas). The letter is the one from the Council of Jerusalem, described in the preceding verses.

We have seen some squabbles previously in *Acts*, but today we see the first real political rift in the church, hardly 20 years after the death of Christ. Paul wants to revisit the cities where he and Barnabas had established new churches the previous year, and Barnabas agrees. But they fall out because Barnabas wants to take John Mark, and Paul does not. So they divide. Barnabas and John Mark sail to Cyprus to visit the new churches there. Paul takes Silas to begin a new mission by land, north to Syria and Galatia (Turkey).

Truth be told, there probably wasn't room in a single group for Paul and Barnabas' egos. It is somewhat startling to see their feet of clay, in the form of pride, interfering with their mission. These are the founders of Christianity, among the bravest and holiest men the earth has seen. They are revered among the greatest saints in liturgical churches and admired as great men and models in more evangelical protestant churches.

And yet, here they are, spatting like a couple of committee members, digging in their heels and, finally, walking away in different directions. It is the first schism! If Paul and Barnabas can't hold it together, what chance do we have?

Very little. Christianity is split into hundreds, if not thousands, of denominations and branches for a reason: Pride is born into us and will be with us until we die.

Pride may be incurable but it is, as doctors say, "treatable." We can monitor and meditate upon our pridefulness, seeking to minimize it. We must pray for the Holy Spirit to teach us humility, the "poverty of spirit" that Christ promised would bring the Kingdom of Heaven to us (Matthew 5:3). We will sometimes stumble, as did Paul and Barnabas, but our confession and repentance are good medicine.

We will be forgiven; but we must not stop trying to live as Christ asked us, just because we expect forgiveness.

Discussion Question: Unity with Other Denominations

I think every denomination I have ever seen has points of systematic theology, of debatable truth in the Bible, and considers other beliefs heresy to the point that they will not worship with people holding the other idea.

Predestination is a good one. Some "Calvinist" or "reformed" churches believe the Bible states the doctrine of absolute predestination (with some good Scriptural support) and that Christ died only for the elect, i.e. those predestined for salvation; other "Arminian" churches believe that humans have free will (also with some good Scriptural support) and Christ died for anyone who chooses to come to Him; and there are complex theologies in-between.

Does your church refuse to admit members who believe in Christ and confess Him, but have different beliefs in theological concepts like predestination, the Trinity, speaking in tongues, etc.? Do you think it is right to do so? How does your belief mesh with the Bible's teachings on Christian unity, such as John 17 and 1 Corinthians 1?

Acts 16 – Second Journey cont'd

Day 69 - Timothy Works with Paul and Silas

Acts 16:1-5

Paul came to Derbe and then to Lystra, where he found a disciple named Timothy, the son of a believing Jewish woman and a Greek father. The brothers in Lystra and Iconium spoke well of him. Paul wanted Timothy to accompany him, so he took him and circumcised him on account of the Jews in that area, for they all knew that his father was a Greek.

As they went from town to town, they delivered the decisions handed down by the apostles and elders in Jerusalem for the people to obey. So the churches were strengthened in the faith and grew daily in numbers.

Commentary

Paul and Barnabas, having had a disagreement, have parted ways and gone on separate missions. Paul is traveling by land, accompanied by Silas (a.k.a. Silvanus), an elder from the church in Jerusalem. But although he takes a land route rather than sailing, Paul returns to three of the towns where he and Barnabas founded churches during his first journey. (See map page 224.)

This, the first leg of the journey through Syria and Cilicia, would have been comparatively easy. Paul's home, Tarsus, was located in Cilicia halfway between Antioch and Derbe. A straight journey would have been about 350 miles, but they wandered from town to town along the way, and they apparently stayed in a number of towns to make new converts and encourage old ones.

Having reached Lystra, Paul meets Timothy, who will become his faithful companion and scribe (and ultimately the leader of the great church in Ephesus). According to Jewish law, one was considered a Jew by birth if his mother was Jewish. Thus, Timothy is a Jew, but for some reason, he had not been circumcised. Paul has the circumcision performed.

Remember, the Council of Jerusalem has just issued a letter holding that circumcision is no longer required. Why would Paul force this painful surgery on his disciple?

The Bible does not tell us, but one might speculate that there was lingering skepticism about accepting Gentiles into Christian churches. Lystra and Derbe were small and comparatively unsophisticated agricultural towns, and Jewish converts dominated the little churches there. So although they had been told to accept Gentiles, individual members would have been more comfortable with other Jewish converts.

Moreover, since Paul intends to travel to new areas to preach in synagogues, it was probably prudent that his company be as Jewish as possible. He could not have brought a Gentile into a synagogue with him, and if he had been suspected of traveling and eating with a Gentile, it would have seriously alienated a Jewish community right off the bat. So, one might speculate that Paul meant to augment Timothy's effectiveness in bringing the gospel to the Jews.

Day 70 - Paul's Vision of the Macedonian

Acts 16:6-10

After the Holy Spirit had prevented them from speaking the word in the province of Asia, they traveled through the region of Phrygia and Galatia. And when they came to the border of Mysia, they tried to enter Bithynia, but the Spirit of Jesus would not permit them. So they passed by Mysia and went down to Troas.

During the night, Paul had a vision of a man of Macedonia standing and pleading with him, "Come over to Macedonia and help us." As soon as Paul had seen the vision, we got ready to leave for Macedonia, concluding that God had called us to preach the gospel to them.

It is here, in Acts 16, that Paul's extraordinary travels to spread Christ's church truly begin. He has reached the farthest points of his previous journey, the minor towns of Iconium, Derbe, and Lystra, where he has met his faithful assistant Timothy and added Timothy to his entourage. This becomes the jumping-off point for him to bring the gospel to Europe.

The details given to us have become sparse in this section. Each sentence may compress months. They travel half the length of Turkey into northern Greece (Macedonia) in the space of today's few verses. And their travels were slow and difficult by today's standards. (In fact, the journey would have been near-impossible except for the *Pax Romana*.)

For as awful as the Roman conquerors were, they were a major improvement over the previous lawless hodgepodge of tribes which would have made travel nearly impossible. The *Pax Romana* — the "Roman peace" — consisted of armies to suppress bandits, and navies to suppress pirates, and the building of roads, and trails, and ports over the entire Mediterranean region. Also, governors to oversee it.

(Both Pompey, in 67 B.C., and Julius Caesar himself, in 75 B.C., utterly annihilated bands of Mediterranean pirates, destroying their ships and crucifying or enslaving the pirate population from Judea to Spain.)

Notice the intriguing shift between the first and third person. The writer sometimes refers to the group as "we" and sometimes as "they." Luke is certainly the author of *Acts*, but was he traveling with Paul in the second journey? Or did he simply piece in another account, perhaps from Timothy? Many scholars believe that the Gentile Luke, who became a devoted follower of Paul, might have been from Troas and joined the group there; this would certainly explain the shift from "they" to "we" when the group leaves Troas.

<u>Note</u>: Luke's gospel was likely written (at least in part) under Paul's direction, perhaps while Paul was in Rome. (See Acts 28:30-31.) Of the three Synoptic Gospels, *Luke* certainly is the most directly aimed at Gentile readers.

Day 71 - The Conversion of Lydia

Acts 16:11-15

We sailed from Troas straight to Samothrace, and the following day on to Neapolis. From there we went to the Roman colony of Philippi, the leading city of that district of Macedonia. And we stayed there several days.

On the Sabbath we went outside the city gate along the river, where it was customary to find a place of prayer. After sitting down, we spoke to the women who had gathered there.

Among those listening was a woman named Lydia, a dealer in purple cloth from the city of Thyatira, who was a worshiper of God. The Lord opened her heart to respond to Paul's message. And when she and her household had been baptized, she urged us, "If you consider me a believer in the Lord, come and stay at my house." And she persuaded us.

Commentary

The names of the places visited on Paul's second journey are becoming downright confusing by now. In broad terms, today's passage recounts that Paul and his troupe sailed from Turkey to northern Greece. It was a trip of 150 miles in a rickety wooden ship.

Note the city of Philippi, the largest city in Macedonia. It is the church founded here to which Paul will later write the *Epistle to the Philippians*.

One might make a long study of Lydia, a fascinating woman. Her influence and power, and Paul's relationship with her, squelch a lot of overstatement about minimalizing women, both in Roman society and in the Bible.

Paul goes to the river specifically to convert the women there. Lydia is an independent woman, with a successful business, rich enough to have a large house and a "household" which follows her. And she is secure enough to invite a group of traveling men to stay with her.

We see here, and in several places, an unexplained worship of "God" outside of Judaism proper. We will, in fact, be introduced to adherents of John the Baptist in a few chapters. Leading us to ask: how much interesting religious and cultural history has been lost forever? 99.9%? And how much more would have been lost without Luke's record that we can still read today?

So we must appreciate the *Acts of the Apostles* not only as a unique history of the Christian church, but also as a fascinating history of the Greek world 2,000 years ago.

Day 72 - Paul and Silas in Prison

Acts 16:16-24

One day as we were going to the place of prayer, we were met by a slave girl with a spirit of divination, who earned a large income for her masters by fortune-telling. This girl followed Paul and the rest of us, shouting, "These men are servants of the Most High God, who are proclaiming to you the way of salvation!"

She continued this for many days. Eventually Paul grew so aggravated that he turned and said to the spirit, "In the name of Jesus Christ I command you to come out of her!" And the spirit left her at that very moment.

When the girl's owners saw that their hope of making money was gone, they seized Paul and Silas and dragged them before the authorities in the marketplace. They brought them to the magistrates and said, "These men are Jews and are throwing our city into turmoil by promoting customs that are unlawful for us Romans to adopt or practice."

The crowd joined in the attack against Paul and Silas, and the magistrates ordered that they be stripped and beaten with rods. And after striking them with many blows, they threw them into prison and ordered the jailer to guard them securely. On receiving this order, he placed them in the inner cell and fastened their feet in the stocks.

Commentary

Paul was not in Philippi for long before he started causing trouble. Usually, the disturbances he caused began in synagogues, where part of the congregation would be outraged at his heresy, i.e. teaching that Jesus was the Son of God.

But the Jewish population of Philippi was apparently small. There is no mention of a synagogue. Since a synagogue requires only ten Jewish men to convene, and any significant Jewish community will start one, Jewish residents were likely sparse. Also, the crowd's identification of the missionaries as "Jews" tends to show that they were an oddity. Perhaps the Aegean Sea was a choke point for the Jewish diaspora.

Lacking his usual means of raising havoc, Paul does the one thing that is guaranteed to create political action: he hurts the profits of local businessmen. The slave woman, like a gypsy at a fair, was telling fortunes for money. When Paul cast out her spirit, the source of profit was destroyed.

The punishment for this comes quickly because they are outsiders, foreigners, and Jews. If they had been locals, or if the magistrates had known they were Roman citizens, they would have received the benefit of a rudimentary legal process (as we will see in the next few verses).

But the oddest thing about this story is that Paul has silenced a woman because she was following him around, proclaiming that he was bringing salvation from God. One might have thought this would be helpful!

She simply got on his nerves. Paul always struggled with pride, and here, he seems to have stuck his hand in the hornet's nest for a questionable motivation. For whatever reason, he seems to like to cause trouble. Lacking a synagogue to outrage, he has been forced to improvise a way to anger the Greeks.

Discussion Question: Are We Lukewarm?

Paul preaches to the point that people are outraged, and riot, and attack him, and have him arrested. Yet most of the people I know are reluctant to cause the slightest social disturbance by preaching Christ.

Is Christ so forgiving that He will save us when we do not follow His command to preach the Gospel? Or will He see us like the Church of Laodicea, in Revelation 3:15 – "I know your deeds, that you are neither cold nor hot; I wish that you were cold or hot. So because you are lukewarm, and neither hot nor cold, I will spit you out of My mouth."

Day 73 - The Philippian Jailer Converted

Acts 16:25-34

About midnight Paul and Silas were praying and singing hymns to God, and the other prisoners were listening to them. Suddenly a strong earthquake shook the foundations of the prison. At once all the doors flew open and everyone's chains came loose.

When the jailer woke up and saw the prison doors open, he drew his sword and was about to kill himself, presuming that the prisoners had escaped. But Paul called out in a loud voice, "Do not harm yourself! We are all here!"

Calling for lights, the jailer rushed in and fell trembling before Paul and Silas. Then he brought them out and asked, "Sirs, what must I do to be saved?"

They replied, "Believe in the Lord Jesus and you will be saved, you and your household." Then Paul and Silas spoke the word of the Lord to him and to everyone in his house. At that hour of the night, the jailer took them and washed their wounds. And without delay, he and all his household were baptized. Then he brought them into his home and set a meal before them. So he and all his household rejoiced that they had come to believe in God.

Commentary

Richard Lovelace, a British poet, wrote: "Stone walls do not a prison make/Nor iron bars a cage," and it never applied more literally to anyone than to Peter and Paul. They escape ambushes and prisons time after time.

In Acts 5, an angel opens the doors of a prison in Jerusalem, releasing Peter and the other apostles; in Acts 9, Paul escapes Damascus by being lowered over the wall in a basket; in Acts 12, an angel releases Peter from Herod's prison and leads him out of the city gates past sleeping guards. In today's lesson, God simply smacks the prison with an earthquake.

Of all the escapes, this one is the most symbolic. Christ promised that "the truth will set you free" (John 8:32) and likened his death to the destruction of the Temple. Paul and Silas' escape is a dramatic physical reminder of our spiritual release from the prison of sin. By the power of God and through their belief in Him, their earthly shackles fall away and the prison doors fall open.

Fittingly, the prison guard who witnesses these events is converted in a rush, much as the scales fell from Paul's eyes in Acts 9:18; the door to salvation is opened to him just as those who heard Christ's words were freed. Both the apostles and their jailer are set free.

Note that the jailer is about to kill himself. We remember that Herod executed the jailers when Peter escaped in Acts 12:19. Being a jailer was apparently a risky career path.

Day 74 - Paul and Silas Released from Prison

Acts 16:35-40

When daylight came, the magistrates sent their officers with the order: "Release those men."

The jailer informed Paul: "The magistrates have sent orders to release you. Now you may go on your way in peace."

But Paul said to the officers, "They beat us publicly without a trial and threw us into prison, even though we are Roman citizens. And now do they want to send us away secretly? Absolutely not! Let them come themselves and escort us out!"

So the officers relayed this message to the magistrates, who were alarmed to hear that Paul and Silas were Roman citizens. They came to appease them and led them out, requesting that they leave the city. After Paul and Silas came out of the prison, they went to Lydia's house to see the brothers and encourage them. Then they left the city.

Commentary

Paul's bit of pridefulness shows through again here. You can almost hear him saying, "They can't treat me like this. I'm a Roman citizen!" And indeed, both he and Silas have been treated incorrectly under Roman law, as if they are a couple of wandering Jews of no account rather than citizens.

An important character in all of this is Lydia, who is barely mentioned. Unlike the other cities of Macedonia, Philippi will have a house, courtesy of Lydia, to serve as a center of worship and meeting, and she herself no doubt would keep it ready to receive converts.

It is fortunate that Philippi will have such a solid church because it is the center of a large district. The Roman Province of Macedonia was much larger than one thinks of it today. Due to the lasting effects of Alexander the Great, it included nearly all of Greece except the Peloponnesian peninsula, and all or parts of modern-day Bulgaria, Macedonia, and Serbia. Founding an active and continuing church in Philippi was critical for the spread of Christianity to the north.

Bonus Discussion: "Brothers" in Greek

There is a translation issue in Greek with the word "brother," which in Greek is *adelphos*, and more specifically with its plural form *adelphoi*.

The word does indeed have a primary meaning of "brother/brothers." But in Christianity, "brothers" extends beyond biological relationships to denote spiritual kinship among believers. There is a metaphorical or even spiritually-determined familial bond within the Christian community. And in this sense, *adelphoi* is not gender-specific. Without any doubt it includes female believers. A Greek reader would have understood it to be gender-neutral in meaning.

I would prefer the "dynamic equivalent" translation of "brothers and sisters" at times; and the clause "they went to Lydia's house to see the brothers and encourage them" is the most extreme example, since it patently includes Lydia!

Our discussion might also help some readers understand the difference between the terms "literal" (or "word-for-word") translation and "dynamic equivalent" translation. The first would always translate "*adelphoi*" to "brothers," because that is the literal translation. A "dynamic equivalent" translation would say "brothers and sisters" because that more accurately conveys what the author intended.

We can make up the difference, however, when we read a more literal translation, for most of us (hopefully) understand that "brothers" in the Bible most often is a gender-neutral term.

(And for you language nerds, yes, in this passage the Greek word used is not literally *adelphoi*, but the plural accusative *adelphous*. Like other inflected languages, Greek words change form sometimes depending on their function in a sentence.)

Acts 17 – Paul Reaches Greece

Day 75 - Paul and Silas in Thessalonica

Acts 17:1-9

When they had passed through Amphipolis and Apollonia, they came to Thessalonica, where there was a Jewish synagogue. As was his custom, Paul went into the synagogue, and on three Sabbaths he reasoned with them from the Scriptures, explaining and proving that the Christ had to suffer and rise from the dead. "This Jesus I am proclaiming to you is the Christ," he declared. Some of the Jews were persuaded and joined Paul and Silas, along with a large number of God-fearing Greeks and quite a few leading women.

The Jews, however, became jealous. So they brought in some troublemakers from the marketplace, formed a mob, and sent the city into an uproar. They raided Jason's house in search of Paul and Silas, hoping to bring them out to the people. But when they could not find them, they dragged Jason and some other brothers before the city officials, shouting, "These men who have turned the world upside down have now come here, and Jason has welcomed them into his home. They are all defying Caesar's decrees, saying that there is another king, named Jesus!"

On hearing this, the crowd and city officials were greatly disturbed. And they collected bond from Jason and the others, and then released them.

Commentary

Paul and Silas are marching through Macedonia (modern-day northern Greece) like generals on a campaign. (See the map, p. 224-25) Thessalonica was a major port; it still is today, and the modern city of Thessaloniki is the second-largest city in Greece. There Paul and Silas have great success converting both Jews and Gentiles. Although women were silent in synagogues, their importance to the creation of this church is highlighted by their specific mention.

The resistance to Christian conversion is growing. To engage the power of the Roman authorities, the Jewish leaders attempt to convince them that Jesus is a temporal king, and therefore Paul and Silas are political enemies of Rome.

Rome allowed an unusual degree of religious freedom to conquered territories, but any sign of political rebellion was dealt with swiftly and harshly. So the enemies of Christianity attempted to convince Roman authorities that Christianity was a political party, rather than a religion, just as Caiaphas had attempted to convince Pilate that Christ had set himself up as the "King of the Jews."

The events show an unusual respect for the judicial process. These events occurred during the reign of Claudius, a relatively sane and beneficent Roman Emperor; his character is reflected in the fair treatment of the accused. The mob, instead of simply beating and stoning Jason and the unnamed brothers, as they had done to Paul in Lystra (Acts 14:19), take them to the "police"; and the magistrates set them free on bail, pending trial.

Day 76 - Paul and Silas in Berea

Acts 17:10-15

As soon as night had fallen, the brothers sent Paul and Silas away to Berea. On arriving there, they went into the Jewish synagogue. Now the Bereans were more noble-minded than the Thessalonians, for they received the message with great eagerness and examined the Scriptures every day to see if these teachings were true. As a result, many of them believed, along with quite a few prominent Greek women and men.

But when the Jews from Thessalonica learned that Paul was also proclaiming the word of God in Berea, they went there themselves to incite and agitate the crowds. The brothers immediately sent Paul to the coast, but Silas and Timothy remained in Berea. Those who escorted Paul brought him to Athens and then returned with instructions for Silas and Timothy to join him as soon as possible.

Commentary

To recap previous events, in central Anatolia (modern-day Turkey), Paul added Timothy to his retinue. They outraged the Jewish establishment and had to move on, but bypassed what was then called "Asia" (western Turkey today) and sailed all the way to Macedonia.

As had happened in central Anatolia, Paul's teachings have outraged the Jewish establishment in the city of Thessalonica, in Macedonia. Paul's religion is not even a proper Jewish sect: it includes Gentiles. The converted Jews worship and consort openly with non-Jewish Gentiles. This would have been doubly inflammatory, like a social club in the Jim Crow era that included both whites and blacks.

Paul is now a hunted man. Mobs take to the road to find and kill him.

For unknown reasons, the tiny Jewish community in Berea accepts the missionaries. The reaction of the Berean Jews is to study the Scripture in order to verify (or disprove) what Paul has preached. Rather than accepting a new religion or rejecting it out of hand, they try to learn the facts and understand the arguments before making a decision. (The "Berean" movement, started around 1780, emphasizes the need to examine the Bible as the primary tool of theology.)

But the Jews of Berea are an exception; most of those involved in the struggle for Christianity—occurring all the way from the Egyptian border to Athens—have become set in their beliefs. We can see four political/social/religious camps pertinent to the early spread of Christianity and the events described in *Acts*.

First, there is the original Jewish splinter sect that believes that Christ is the Messiah. We associate them with the original apostles and early disciples, particularly Peter and James (the Lesser).

Second is a group of monotheistic Gentiles. They have been attracted to the personal relationship with the One God that Judaism teaches, and they seem to adopt Christ more easily than the actual Jews. Their full acceptance by the Christian Jews has begun to change Christianity from essentially a Jewish sect into a completely new religion. Paul associates himself with this group (although he certainly converts many Jews, as well). This group will come to dominate Rome and, eventually, the entire Western civilization.

Third, ranged against Paul and Silas is the traditional Jewish establishment, which openly wants them arrested, and if possible executed, for heresy. They are joined by a few Gentiles whom Paul has managed to irritate (because of their commercial, rather than religious, concerns).

Fourth, the most powerful political force in the world —Rome itself—is apathetic. Rome has hardly even noticed the new religion. But that is about to change.

In the next section of *Acts*, Christianity will take a huge step forward. Paul will begin to proselytize the general Gentile population directly, by telling them the Greco-Roman gods are false — and unsurprisingly, the Romans will not like it.

Day 77 - The Philosophers at Athens

Acts 17:16-21

While Paul was waiting for them [Timothy and Silas] in Athens, he was deeply disturbed in his spirit to see that the city was full of idols. So he reasoned in the synagogue with the Jews and God-fearing Gentiles, and in the marketplace with those he met each day.

Some Epicurean and Stoic philosophers also began to debate with him. Some of them asked, "What is this babbler trying to say?" Others said, "He seems to be advocating foreign gods." They said this because Paul was proclaiming the good news of Jesus and the resurrection.

So they took Paul and brought him to the Areopagus, where they asked him, "May we know what this new teaching is that you are presenting? For you are bringing some strange notions to our ears, and we want to know what they mean."

Now all the Athenians and foreigners who lived there spent their time doing nothing more than hearing and articulating new ideas.

Commentary

As indicated in the final verse, Athens was still the center of philosophy in 50 A.D.; men gathered outside on a hill called the Areopagus to discuss ideas. It was one of the most concentrated centers of philosophical discussion in the history of the entire world. Paul has made it into the big time! His walking into the Areopagus of Athens was like a baseball player walking into Yankee Stadium.

Although Epicureanism has come to be associated with overindulgence, in fact, the opposite is true. The Epicureans believed in stringent moderation as one key to perfecting human life. They believed that human beings had souls which survived their deaths. And while they believed that gods existed, they thought that these gods were not interested in life on earth and certainly would never intervene in earthly affairs.

The Stoics, remarkably, came very close to agreeing with the fundamental truth of John 1:1 — "In the beginning was the Word, and the Word was with God. And the Word was God." Although they did not call him "God," they believed that the Word, or *logos*, was not simply a force, but a reasoning person; and they had true morals based on the laws of the *logos*.

The Stoics were ethical, tried to live good lives, and believed in the human soul. But they lacked an essential ingredient of salvation: A living relationship with the Word and worship of Him as God, which the Jews were given in the Old Testament. They had no life in the spirit, as we call it.

And so, as close as they had come to truth by using their sheer intellect, the Greeks worshiped statues, to which they had ascribed a vast, rich mythology. But intellect cannot find God; as they are to discover, only the spirit can find God.

Plato and his intellectual descendants (Neo-Platonists) probably got the closest to believing in God; but they are not mentioned in the Bible.

There are a considerable number of people in the Western world, and probably all over the earth, who unwittingly practice a modified (and watered down) version of these ancient philosophies.

<u>Bonus Material: Areopagus</u>

Areopagus is Latin for "Hill of Ares," a site dedicated to the Greek god of war. It was where the council of Athens presided before the Roman conquest; thus, it is the exact spot where modern democracy was invented!

Day 78 - Paul Addresses the Areopagus (1)

Acts 17:22-27

Then Paul stood up in the meeting of the Areopagus and said, "Men of Athens, I see that in every way you are very religious. For as I walked around and examined your objects of worship, I even found an altar with this inscription:

TO AN UNKNOWN GOD

Therefore what you worship as something unknown, I now proclaim to you.

The God who made the world and everything in it is the Lord of heaven and earth and does not live in temples made by human hands. Nor is He served by human hands, as if He needed anything, because He Himself gives everyone life and breath and everything else. From one man He made every nation of men, that they should inhabit the whole earth; and He determined their appointed times and the boundaries of their lands.

God intended that they would seek Him and perhaps reach out for Him and find Him, though He is not far from each one of us.

Commentary

Today's Scripture recounts a monumental day in the history of religion and civilization. If you find it startling to encounter Stoics and Epicureans in the Bible, you are not alone.

I studied Greek philosophy in college, before I ever read the *Book of Acts*. And let me tell you, when I read this passage for the first time, it "blew my mind." Two utterly separate worlds collided in my brain.

Paul connected Jesus to the great intellectual history of Classical civilization.

To see Paul debating with the professional philosophers of Athens is not simply startling. It is like plugging an ancient lamp into a modern electric circuit and watching it light up. The theology of Paul, Jesus, Moses, and even Abraham, becomes directly connected to debates we might hear in a contemporary university discussion.

Moreover, Paul's debate at the Areopagus represents a second revolutionary moment; for this is the first time he has preached the Gospel to polytheists.

The Roman Empire took its culture from Greece, including the Greeks' polytheistic religion. Up until this point, Paul and the other missionaries have converted only those who believed in the Hebrew God (although some were Gentiles). But today, he steps onto the center stage of Greco-Roman philosophy, and tells them—the high priests of logic—that the religion of the mighty Roman Empire is false. For the first time, he tries to convert Romans from their state religion to Christianity.

And it must have been as startling to Greek philosophers in 50 A.D. as it is to us, today. To them, Paul is a hick preacher of a minor religion, from a backwater Semitic province, not a learned Greek scholar. But Paul has enormous power as a speaker and rationalist, driven by the Holy Spirit. He instinctively uses a minor altar dedicated "to the unknown god" as a hook for his argument.

The real force of his argument does not come from Greek logic. Rather, it comes from an emotional and spiritual argument. The very idea of a personal relationship with a living God was unknown to the Greek wise men. Rather than starting with the human mind and seeking to find God with it, Paul tells them that God has found them. They had never heard of such a thing!

It is an argument that will change the world. As we know today, Paul will prevail even over the mighty Roman Empire; over the next 300 years, Rome will slowly become the very center of Christianity.

Day 79 - Paul Addresses the Areopagus (2)

Acts 17:26-28

"From one man He made every nation of men, that they should inhabit the whole earth; and He determined their appointed times and the boundaries of their lands.

God intended that they would seek Him and perhaps reach out for Him and find Him, though He is not far from each one of us. 'For in Him we live and move and have our being.' As some of your own poets have said, 'We are His offspring.'"

Commentary

Paul continues his spectacular speech to the Greek philosophers by explaining how and why humanity was created. We were created by a single God, and the purpose of our lives is to find our way to Him. He dwells close to us, where He may be easily found.

Paul's rhetorical training is limited compared to his audience, for he is speaking to the most sophisticated philosophers in the Western World. Luckily, he is thoroughly grounded in the use of precedent. Proof by precedent—showing that one's argument is supported by accepted ancient authorities—is the fundamental method of argument used in Judaism. Although the Greeks did not lean on ancient scholars as much as the Jews leaned on the Bible and Mosaic Law, they recognized precedent as a valid form of argument.

("Rhetoric" in this sense refers to a formal set of skills and rules for making convincing arguments; up until about 80 years ago, Rhetoric was taught as a formal subject in English-speaking high schools.)

Paul also shows some serious non-Hebrew education, because he recites a line— "For we are indeed his offspring"—from a popular work of Greek philosophy, the *Phaenomena* of Aratus. *Phaenomena* means "appearances." The *Phaenomena* of Aratus was a philosophical/astrological work describing the "appearance" of the constellations. Every educated Greek listener would have known it.

So Paul's argument here fit comfortably within the parameters of the Athenians' philosophical inquiry. In his next words, however, Paul will say things that will amaze and confound them.

Bonus Discussion: Philosophy and Christianity

In his work, Aratus stated that Zeus had created the universe, including mankind. This theory was at odds with the accepted Greek mythology. But some Greek philosophers (Plato, to name the most famous, and the Stoics in general) had already begun to ponder the possibility that there was one god who created the universe.

Plato and the Stoics called this driving force of the universe the *logos*, or the Word. Their ideas were very close to John 1:1, "In the beginning was the Word." And in fact, the word "Word" in our Bible (specifically in John 1:1) is a translation of the Greek word *logos*.

In today's Scripture, Paul has shown the intimidating scholars of the Greek Areopagus that he belongs on the speakers' podium. He has successfully shown the crowd—and it is a very critical crowd indeed! —that there is ample precedent in Greek philosophy for the idea that one god created all humanity and continues to take an interest in our lives.

But although Plato, and even more the Neo-Platonists who further developed his ideas, seemed always on the brink of finding monotheism through their intelligence, they never did. Salvation came from a scruffy tribe of herdsman in Judea, who sought God with their hearts and spirits, rather than their minds.

We mentioned 1 Corinthians 1 in the discussion of Christian unity, but the chapter also brilliantly describes the inability of either Greek philosophers or Jewish mystics to find the secret of salvation.

Day 80 - Paul Addresses the Areopagus (3)

Acts 17:29-34

"Therefore, being offspring of God, we should not think that the Divine Being is like gold or silver or stone, an image formed by man's skill and imagination.

Although God overlooked the ignorance of earlier times, He now commands all people everywhere to repent. For He has set a day when He will judge the world with justice by the Man He has appointed. He has given proof of this to everyone by raising Him from the dead."

When they heard about the resurrection of the dead, some began to mock him, but others said, "We want to hear you again on this topic." At that, Paul left the Areopagus. But some joined him and believed, including Dionysius the Areopagite, a woman named Damaris, and others who were with them.

Commentary

In Acts 17:22-28, Paul stood up and began to address the assemblage to teach them that there is but one God, who created everything in the universe, including the earth and humanity. Today, finally, he tells them something that nobody has told them before: their gods do not exist. They are just statues. They are "an image formed by the imagination . . . of man." There is a true God, who has sent a man to save them from death, and as a sign has been raised up from the dead.

Moreover, God now expects them to repent of their ignorant polytheistic blasphemy; He is going to judge them for it. And as proof, the Man appointed for the task has been resurrected from the dead!

The concepts are astonishing to them. Several listeners are converted on the spot, and some number of others are interested in hearing more. Some openly laugh at him and simply dismiss him. But the turning point has been reached. The Gospel has been revealed, openly and forcefully, to the mainstream intelligentsia of the Roman Empire.

Acts 18 – Second Journey Ends, Third Journey Begins

Day 81 - Paul in Corinth (1)

Acts 18:1-8

After this, Paul left Athens and went to Corinth. There he found a Jew named Aquila, a native of Pontus, who had recently come from Italy with his wife Priscilla because Claudius had ordered all the Jews to leave Rome. Paul went to visit them, and he stayed and worked with them because they were tentmakers by trade, just as he was.

Every Sabbath he reasoned in the synagogue, trying to persuade Jews and Greeks alike. And when Silas and Timothy came down from Macedonia, Paul devoted himself fully to the word, testifying to the Jews that Jesus is the Christ. But when they opposed and insulted him, he shook out his garments and told them, "Your blood be on your own heads! I am innocent of it. From now on I will go to the Gentiles."

So Paul left the synagogue and went next door to the house of Titus Justus, a worshiper of God. Crispus, the synagogue leader, and his whole household believed in the Lord. And many of the Corinthians who heard the message believed and were baptized.

Commentary

Following his adventure debating the philosophers of Athens, Paul heads west to the city of Corinth. He stays at first with Aquila and Priscilla, Italian Jews who, like many Jews to come, had been expelled from their country by a villainous ruler. He then gets upset because so many Jews are resisting conversion. He thus moves in with a Gentile family, declaring that the Jews of the synagogue can—in effect—go to hell. Notice the Semitic idiom of his "shaking out his garments."

(Compare Matthew 10:14, where Jesus tells His disciples that, if people reject their teaching, "take back your *blessing of* peace. And whoever does not receive you nor listen to your words, as you leave that house or city, *shake the dust off* your feet.")

We get some insight into Paul's method of travel. Unlike most pilgrims, Paul is not carrying a large sum of money to pay for his trip, nor is he asking for donations. He is working his way. Traditionally, Christians attribute tent-making to Paul. We cannot be 100% sure of his trade, however, because the Greek word refers both to leather workers generally, as well as tent makers.

So let's just say his trade was making leather tents, and he moves in with Aquila because he is also a leather worker. No doubt this was advantageous to Paul; Aquila would have places to buy leather and supplies, and contacts to sell finished products, and a space for Paul to work.

Although making tents from leather might seem odd today, it was very popular 2,000 years ago. Canvas and goat hair were also used but did not hold up as well. Leather is good for traveling because it is pliable and so easy to set up and take down, and it is rain-resistant. The Roman army used leather tents almost exclusively.

Jews probably did not tan much leather, which is difficult to do while following Mosaic law, so Paul would have bought his skins already tanned. Their leather was primarily goat and calfskin, which are "clean" animals and make light leathers.

Today, some Christians use the word "tentmaker" to describe people who function in Christian ministries but receive little or no pay for church work, getting their livelihood from unrelated work.

Day 82 - Paul in Corinth (2)

Acts 18:9-17

One night the Lord spoke to Paul in a vision: "Do not be afraid; keep on speaking; do not be silent. For I am with you and no one will lay a hand on you, because I have many people in this city." So Paul stayed for a year and a half, teaching the word of God among the Co-rinthians.

While Gallio was proconsul of Achaia, the Jews coordinated an at-tack on Paul and brought him before the judgment seat. "This man is persuading the people to worship God in ways contrary to the law," they said.

But just as Paul was about to speak, Gallio told the Jews, "If this matter involved a wrongdoing or vicious crime, O Jews, it would be reasonable for me to hear your complaint. But since it is a dispute about words and names and your own law, settle it yourselves. I refuse to be a judge of such things." And he drove them away from the judgment seat.

At this, the crowd seized Sosthenes the synagogue leader and beat him in front of the judgment seat. But none of this was of concern to Gallio.

Commentary

Today's Scripture hints at the size and importance of Corinth. It had been a great city-state in Greece for hundreds of years before the Roman conquest, and it would become home to one of the great churches of antiquity.

Roman attitudes towards Christianity and other religions in Ro-man colonies had not changed since the Crucifixion. The religious practices of conquered peoples did not concern them. Rome's attitude towards its gods was that they should be appeased to help Rome; con-quered peoples could believe whatever and worship whomever they pleased, as long as they didn't cause trouble. In particular, Roman au-thorities were generally unconcerned with a peculiar little Jewish sect, which had not shown any inclination to dabble in politics.

When the Jews caused problems in the streets of Rome, Caligula simply expelled them all. But he didn't interfere in their beliefs. Of course, this will change. Paul has not yet gone to Rome!

It was during this period, while Paul was in Corinth, that he wrote the first epistles that appear in the Bible, two long letters to the little church in Thessalonica (*Thessalonians 1 and 2*).

The chronology of the New Testament is a bit out of whack after the Gospels; all of Paul's epistles (and probably the non-Pauline epistles) were written during the time period covered by the *Book of Acts*, and they do not appear in order of when they were written. So for example, *1 and 2 Thessalonians* were written many years before *Romans*.

Day 83 - Paul Returns to Antioch — The End of Paul's Second Journey

Acts 18:18-23

Paul remained in Corinth for quite some time before saying goodbye to the brothers. He had his head shaved in Cenchrea to keep a vow he had made, and then he sailed for Syria, accompanied by Priscilla and Aquila.

When they reached Ephesus, Paul parted ways with Priscilla and Aquila. He himself went into the synagogue there and reasoned with the Jews. When they asked him to stay for a while longer, he declined. But as he left, he said, "I will come back to you if God is willing." And he set sail from Ephesus.

When Paul had landed at Caesarea, he went up and greeted the church at Jerusalem. Then he went down to Antioch.

After Paul had spent some time in Antioch, he traveled from place to place throughout the region of Galatia and Phrygia, strengthening all the disciples.

Commentary

Paul ends his second journey by traveling fairly quickly all the way from Corinth, in modern-day Greece, back to Antioch. (It is during this stay in Antioch that Paul writes his *Epistle to the Galatians*.) He lands briefly in Ephesus with a promise to come back – a promise he will keep.

Instead of taking the shorter and safer route along the Anatolian coast back to Antioch, he sails all the way south to Caesarea. He "went up to greet the church." You might have noticed that, in *Acts*, "up" often means south or east, towards Jerusalem, and "down" can mean north. Perhaps this is because Jerusalem is the center of Judaism, or perhaps because it is in the mountains – "uphill."

Paul cuts his hair because of a vow he had taken; it seems odd, because this is the first we have heard of it. At some point during the journey Paul has apparently taken a Nazarite vow. If you are familiar with Samson, you will know who the Nazirites were. (If you are interested, the source of the Nazirite vows is Numbers 6.)

It was not uncommon for devout Jews, even in this later time, to take temporary Nazirite vows, generally from 30 to 100 days. The law under Numbers 6 requires a ritual cleansing and blessing at the Temple to perfect the vow. Paul will do this later (in Acts 21:22-26).

We have seen Judaism and Christianity becoming increasingly separated in *Acts*, even during Paul's second journey. By the end of this journey, they are properly different religions. Yet, Paul takes a very old-fashioned Mosaic vow that requires a sacrifice at the Temple. So we might conclude that Christians need not follow Judaism, but they can if they want to.

This continued reverence of the Old Testament, despite the break between Judaism and Christianity, will become important in time. A powerful heretical sect of Christ worshippers, the Gnostics, will soon arise; they will reject God's word as revealed in the Old Testament, write and follow various unattested books about Christ's life that differ greatly from the New Testament, and strive against the Pauline Christians for control of Christian belief.

The myriad errors of Gnosticism and the struggles to overcome them are far beyond the scope of this book. It still crops up regularly as an alternative to Christianity; one recent example was the popular fictional work, *The Da Vinci Code*. More importantly, Gnostic principles constantly worm their way into uninformed discussions of Christian doctrine.

Paul's continued attentiveness to Mosaic law—when it is not inconsistent with Christ's teachings—will allow later generations to place Christ in proper context; it is absolutely critical to remember that He was the Messiah prophesied in the Old Testament. And as long as we do not look to it as the source of our salvation, there is generally no harm in following various Old Testament laws.

Please note, "following" does not mean "judging" or "enforcing." We avoid adultery; but we do not kill adulterers. (John 8:1-11)

Day 84 - Apollos Goes to Ephesus

Acts 18:23-28

After Paul had spent some time in Antioch, he traveled from place to place throughout the region of Galatia and Phrygia, strengthening all the disciples.

Meanwhile a Jew named Apollos, a native of Alexandria, came to Ephesus. He was an eloquent man, well versed in the Scriptures. He had been instructed in the way of the Lord and was fervent in spirit. He spoke and taught accurately about Jesus, though he knew only the baptism of John. And he began to speak boldly in the synagogue. When Priscilla and Aquila heard him, they took him in and explained to him the way of God more accurately.

When Apollos resolved to cross over to Achaia, the brothers encouraged him and wrote to the disciples there to welcome him. On his arrival, he was a great help to those who by grace had believed. For he powerfully refuted the Jews in public debate, proving from the Scriptures that Jesus is the Christ.

Commentary

Acts segues abruptly from Paul's second journey to his third; the only indication of a break is a few words that say he spent some time in Antioch, then departed for Galatia and Phrygia. After telling us about Paul's departure, the narrative shifts focus immediately, describing the second-generation missionaries Aquila, Priscilla, and Apollos. This makes the narrative a bit hard to follow, but we will pick back up with Paul himself tomorrow.

There is no more mention of Paul's work in central Anatolia; when we see him again, it will be in the western port city of Ephesus, where he will spend three years. After all, he promised them that he would return and stay a "little longer"!

The bulk of today's Scripture describes the growth of a second generation of Christian teachers and missionaries. They come from all over the Roman world to the new centers of Christianity. Priscilla and Aquila, who were Italian but forced to emigrate to Corinth because they were Jewish, have studied and devoted themselves to Christ so thoroughly that they founded one of the most important churches of the ancient world, Ephesus. Paul had previously stopped briefly in Ephesus — a major seaport — but apparently, he had not founded a church there. Aquila and Priscilla likely worked on their own to found and expand a Christian community.

We do not have a hint as to why Apollos comes to Ephesus. We must assume that the Holy Spirit guided him.

"Achaia" (or Achaea) refers to an important southern region of Greece. Corinth was its capital.

Acts 19 – Paul in Ephesus

Day 85 - Paul in Ephesus (1)

Acts 19:1-7

While Apollos was at Corinth, Paul passed through the interior and came to Ephesus. There he found some disciples and asked them, "Did you receive the Holy Spirit when you became believers?"

"No," they answered, "we have not even heard that there is a Holy Spirit."

"Into what, then, were you baptized?" Paul asked.

"The baptism of John," they replied.

Paul explained: "John's baptism was a baptism of repentance. He told the people to believe in the One coming after him, that is, in Jesus."

On hearing this, they were baptized into the name of the Lord Jesus. And when Paul laid his hands on them, the Holy Spirit came upon them, and they spoke in tongues and prophesied. There were about twelve men in all.

Commentary

Our information about the early church in Ephesus before Paul's second visit is almost non-existent. On his second missionary journey, he visited Ephesus for the first time, but just an overnight stop. He did nothing more than drop off Priscilla and Aquila and promise to return. He was anxious to get back to Antioch after his long sojourn through Macedonia and Greece.

In today's passage, Priscilla and Aquila are not mentioned. Possibly they had converted the handful of disciples Paul encounters; but only when Paul arrives do the unnamed group of believers receive the Holy Spirit, when Paul baptizes them. Recall the words of John the Baptist, "I baptize you with water for repentance. But after me will come one who . . . will baptize you with the Holy Spirit and with fire." (Matthew 3:11)

If they had been baptized by John the Baptist, they were fairly old, for it would have occurred well over 20 years previously. John the Baptist was beheaded around 30 A.D., and Paul arrived in Ephesus around 53 A.D.

Finding followers of John the Baptist in Ephesus is startling and hard to explain. Ephesus is over 1,000 miles from Jerusalem, by land. John has been dead for over 20 years. Has this group been waiting in isolation since the days of John the Baptist? How have they never heard of the Holy Spirit?

Perhaps the "baptism of John" refers to the practice of baptism as initiated by John, not actual baptism by John himself, and this practice had been handed down and spread as a religion. There is so much we do not know about religious practices 2,000 years ago. In *Acts*, we have seen Gentiles worshipping God, Samaritans practicing a different form of Judaism, and now apparently a sect following John the Baptist. And in Paul's epistles, we will discern myriad heretical Gospel sects.

The little Christian churches of this period must have felt isolated. They were separated by vast distances and tied together with only an occasional visit from one of the apostles or brothers. Otherwise, they had almost no communication except for a rare letter, especially if they were inland where travelers were less common. (So if you ever feel isolated by modern secular society, just think back to the believers of Ephesus!)

Now that Paul has come back, things are about to kick into high gear. His visit to Ephesus, lasting over two years, will form the heart of his third journey. And as we will see shortly, the prior disruptions caused by Paul were small potatoes, compared to the uproar he will cause in Ephesus.

Day 86 - Paul in Ephesus (2)

Acts 19:8-10

Then Paul went into the synagogue and spoke boldly there for three months, arguing persuasively about the kingdom of God. But when some of them stubbornly refused to believe and publicly maligned the Way, Paul took his disciples and left the synagogue to conduct daily discussions in the lecture hall of Tyrannus. This continued for two years, so that everyone who lived in the province of Asia, Jews and Greeks alike, heard the word of the Lord.

Commentary

As happened in Corinth previously, Paul begins his teaching in a synagogue but quickly runs into trouble. Having done his best to convince the Jews first, he withdraws and concentrates on the Gentiles. He finds a welcome in the school of a Greek philosopher named "Tyrannus" (not a promising sounding name!).

Paul's travels can get a bit overwhelming and confusing. The *Book of Acts* has a lot of history compressed into a small space and most of it is untaught outside of Bible study classes. The names of people and places are confusing, the political and sociological geography has changed (especially in Turkey and Syria), and the events span a period of roughly 24 years.

So to orient ourselves: Paul made four major journeys. Today, we are in the middle of the third, and it might be a good idea to recap what has gone on so far.

The first journey, made with Barnabas, was the shortest of the three we have studied. It lasted about two years. Paul sailed from Antioch (in Syria, the home of the greatest church in Christendom outside Jerusalem) to the island of Cyprus, in the eastern Mediterranean. He walked across the island from east to west, founding churches in several cities.

He then sailed north to central Turkey and traveled around the provinces known as Cilicia and Galatia; this area was culturally part of Greece at that time (and, of course, politically part of Rome). Quite a bit is written about Paul's adventures in this area, notably the towns of

Perga, Derbe, Lystra, Iconium, and "Antioch in Pisidia," in Acts 13-14. He then backtracked to the coast and sailed back to Antioch (in Syria), where he stayed for several years.

The second journey, which was to last three years, began when he walked from Antioch to Galatia, to visit the mainland churches he founded on his first journey.

He then struck out northwest across the entire length of Turkey and sailed across the Aegean Sea to Philippi, in northern Greece (then called Macedonia). From Philippi, he traveled by land down the length of Greece to Corinth and Athens, both of which were major events. From Athens, he went to Ephesus, then Jerusalem, and then home to Antioch on foot.

We are now at the beginning of Paul's third journey. Paul had left Aquila and Priscilla (Jews who had been expelled from Italy) behind in Ephesus, and his first order of business is to return there. At this point, the Bible tells us simply that he stayed in Ephesus for two years and spread the word to "all of Asia." "Asia" here meant western Turkey, where Ephesus was located; the name "Asia" would not be applied to the world's largest continent until many centuries later.

Remember, the Holy Spirit had specifically instructed Paul to avoid Asia and Bithynia on his second journey. (Acts 16:4-8)

Day 87 - Paul Works Miracles in Ephesus

Acts 19:11-12

God did extraordinary miracles through the hands of Paul, so that even handkerchiefs and aprons that had touched him were taken to the sick, and the diseases and evil spirits left them.

Commentary

The short verse today describes healing by Paul in Ephesus, so extreme that his handkerchief would heal the sick. We saw a similar phenomenon earlier: people came to Jerusalem to be healed by Peter's shadow in Acts 5:12-16. This creates a difficult issue for the 21st-century Christian. If Peter and Paul were able to heal the sick so readily, why do Christians today often remain ill and sometimes die of such illnesses, despite all prayers for healing?

There are countless questions one might ask, and countless answers one might give. But the simplest answer is that nobody knows for sure. We grow accustomed to thinking that our brains can grasp truth; it is the assumption of many scientists that the human mind can understand everything. But it cannot. Our minds and our concept of knowledge are limited.

Christ came to earth to tell us what we need to know in order to satisfy God and find eternal salvation (and then to accomplish a needed sacrifice). He did not tell us everything that God knows or everything that God plans. He came as a human, to tell us what little we are able to grasp as humans.

Imagine an adult attempting to explain an automobile to a small child. The adult will use baby talk and try to simplify his explanation to a level that a child can understand.

Just so, we are God's children, and He has told us the truth in terms we can understand. But we cannot really know the mind of God. We aren't smart enough.

Children fasten their seat belts, get shots from the doctor, don't play with fire or guns, and don't talk to strangers, even though they only partly understand why; their reward is safety, health, and life. They have <u>faith</u> in their parents. Similarly, God's children follow His rules, even though we do not and cannot fully understand everything. We trust that God does understand everything and loves us enough to tell us what to do, to find life.

Nobody said this more eloquently than Paul himself in 1 Corinthians 13: "For now we see in a mirror dimly, but then face to face. Now I know in part; then I shall know fully, even as I have been fully known."

God had a purpose in making Paul such a miraculous healer, which purpose was not told to us. But we learn from the *Gospel of John* that Jesus' miracles were "signs," single events to introduce Jesus as the Son of God, to give Him credibility as the Messiah. But only a few — *John* recounts only seven miracles — because Jesus did not come to save our bodies by miracles, but rather our souls, by faith.

So perhaps we might understand the great healing miracles of Paul and Peter as signs that they carry the gospel from God. Paul healed, not as a promise that those who found Christ would never become sick in their bodies. Rather, Paul healed as a sign, as proof of supernatural power, that through Christ death could be conquered.

Day 88 - Paul in Ephesus—The Sons of Sceva

Acts 19:13-20

Now there were some itinerant Jewish exorcists who tried to invoke the name of the Lord Jesus over those with evil spirits. They would say, "I bind you by Jesus, whom Paul proclaims." Seven sons of Sceva, a Jewish chief priest, were doing this.

Eventually, one of the evil spirits answered them, "Jesus I know, and I know about Paul, but who are you?" Then the man with the evil spirit jumped on them and overpowered them all. The attack was so violent that they ran out of the house naked and wounded.

This became known to all the Jews and Greeks living in Ephesus, and fear came over all of them. So the name of the Lord Jesus was held in high honor. Many who had believed now came forward, confessing and disclosing their deeds. And a number of those who had practiced magic arts brought their books and burned them in front of everyone. When the value of the books was calculated, the total came to fifty thousand drachmas. So the word of the Lord powerfully continued to spread and prevail.

Commentary

The colorful lesson today illustrates the triumph of religion over superstition and the victory of the Holy Spirit over all the unnatural creatures of the world. The Spirit will not allow Jesus' name to be used as some sort of magic talisman by the equivalent of witch doctors, posing as priests. Belief in the word of spiritualists is a perversion of our natural instinct to find God.

The sons of Sceva learn that the power of magic and superstition is illusory, and they learn it the hard way. Selling Jesus as a magic potion backfires on them. It is a great moment for the people of Ephesus because the lesson is not lost on them. Hordes of phony magicians and spiritual healers abandon their wrongful ways, confess their lies, and burn their "magic" books.

Day 89 - The Riot in Ephesus (1)

Acts 19:21-27

After these things had happened, Paul resolved in the Spirit to go to Jerusalem after he had passed through Macedonia and Achaia. "After I have been there," he said, "I must see Rome as well." He sent two of his helpers, Timothy and Erastus, to Macedonia, while he stayed for a time in the province of Asia.

About that time there arose a great disturbance about the Way. It began with a silversmith named Demetrius who made silver shrines of Artemis, bringing much business to the craftsmen.

Demetrius assembled the craftsmen, along with the workmen in related trades. "Men," he said, "you know that this business is our source of prosperity. And you can see and hear that not only in Ephesus, but in nearly the whole province of Asia, Paul has persuaded a great number of people to turn away. He says that man-made gods are no gods at all.

There is danger not only that our business will fall into disrepute, but also that the temple of the great goddess Artemis will be discredited and her majesty deposed—she who is worshiped by all the province of Asia and the whole world."

Commentary

It is tempting to see Demetrius as greedy and a bit silly—nothing more than protecting his job of building silver items to honor a lesser Greek deity; but studying first-century Ephesus sheds a different light.

The Temple of Artemis, in Ephesus, was one of the Seven Wonders of the World. It was four times the size of the Parthenon and must have been a magnificent and awe-inspiring sight. Moreover, it was ancient. The temple of Paul's time was probably the third Temple of Artemis on the site; like St. Paul's Cathedral in London, it was destroyed several times and then rebuilt, larger and more magnificent each time. Nobody knows when the first temple was built, but it was probably sometime around 1,000 B.C.

It is a shame that the temple was destroyed around 400 A.D. It would have ranked with the Taj Mahal and the Great Wall of China as one of the top tourist destinations in the world.

It was not only an architectural masterpiece, but also the center of life in the city and one of the most important centers of Greek culture. Numerous festivals were held there, with games, theater, markets, etc. Young Greeks would travel there to find a spouse!

In a word, the Temple of Artemis was the greatest architectural achievement of Greek civilization. Its size, splendor, antiquity, and cultural importance were unequaled. Understanding this, we can understand the magnitude of the Ephesians' reaction when they believed it to be under threat from Paul's teaching.

Paul's attack on it might be purely theological, but the reaction seems to be more cultural and commercial.

Day 90 - The Riot in Ephesus (2)

Acts 19:28-34

When the men heard this, they were enraged and began shouting, "Great is Artemis of the Ephesians!" Soon the whole city was in disarray. They rushed together into the theatre, dragging with them Gaius and Aristarchus, Paul's traveling companions from Macedonia.

Paul wanted to go before the assembly, but the disciples would not allow him. Even some of Paul's friends who were officials of the province of Asia sent word to him, begging him not to venture into the theatre.

Meanwhile the assembly was in turmoil. Some were shouting one thing and some another, and most of them did not even know why they were there. The Jews in the crowd pushed Alexander forward to explain himself, and he motioned for silence so he could make his defense to the people. But when they realized that he was a Jew, they all shouted in unison for about two hours: "Great is Artemis of the Ephesians!"

Commentary

Demetrius the silversmith has started a proper riot, indeed. The importance of the Great Temple of Artemis is so great that it does not take much in the way of a threat to create hysteria. And like most spontaneous riots, it is utter confusion mixed with enormous potential for violence.

The man named Alexander is a Jew, and almost certainly not a Christian. The Jews are justifiably afraid that this unfocused riot will turn on them because, like the Christians, they consider the Temple of Artemis to be profane.

Ironically, however, it is not their fault. The Jews kept their religion pretty much to themselves. They would not have entered the Temple of Artemis or made idols for it, but they would not have been trying to convince Gentile worshippers that the Temple was unclean and evil. Judaism does not have the strong duty to proselytize that Christianity has; in fact, Judaism was more likely to exclude other tribes and races than to try to convert them. It is Paul and his companions — who are after all "Jewish" by birth, language, and appearance — who have been openly preaching against the worship of idols and trying to convert Gentiles.

This will hardly be the last time that the Jews get blamed for something they didn't do. But do not miss an important development: the violent opposition to Christianity has begun to originate more from Gentiles than from Jews.

Bonus Discussion: Ephesus Today

One of the greatest archeological restorations in world history is being accomplished by the government of Turkey, which has unearthed and restored an enormous number of ancient buildings and roads in Ephesus. There is even a lone pillar from the Temple of Artemis still standing, about a mile from the restored city. If you are in a position to travel overseas, I would encourage you to visit Ephesus, for it is a fantastic site.

This was one of the great cities of its day. It was a seaport, but silting has filled in the harbor and Ephesus now sits about five miles inland from the Aegean Sea and about a 25-minute drive from the port of Kusadasi. A number of cruises call at Kusadasi.

There are also bus tours of the cities Paul visited, for those who really want to get serious about it! Turkey is a good tourist country for Americans; it's safe enough and the food is good, and the last time I was there they liked Americans.

Day 91 - The Riot in Ephesus (3)

Acts 19:35-41

Finally the city clerk quieted the crowd and declared, "Men of Ephesus, doesn't everyone know that the city of Ephesus is guardian of the temple of the great Artemis and of her image, which fell from heaven? Since these things are undeniable, you ought to be calm and not do anything rash. For you have brought these men here, though they have neither robbed our temple nor blasphemed our goddess.

So if Demetrius and his fellow craftsmen have a complaint against anyone, the courts are open and proconsuls are available. Let them bring charges against one another there. But if you are seeking anything beyond this, it must be settled in a legal assembly. For we are in jeopardy of being charged with rioting for today's events, and we have no justification to account for this commotion."

After he had said this, he dismissed the assembly.

Commentary

Roman law and order saves both the Christians and the Jews in Ephesus. It is an ironic moment, because just as the mob fear, the words spoken by Paul will eventually destroy the magnificent Temple of Artemis; in 400 A.D. a Christian emperor will ban the worship of Artemis, and the Temple—one of the Seven Wonders of the World—will be pulled down and destroyed by mobs of people who will loot the very marble until nothing is left standing.

We find out in this passage just how superstitious the Greeks could be, for the great Temple is dedicated to a "sacred stone that fell from the sky" — they are worshipping a meteorite!

Acts 20 – Third Journey - Paul Heads for Home

Day 92 - Paul Returns to Macedonia

Acts 20:1-6

When the uproar had ended, Paul sent for the disciples. And after encouraging them, he said goodbye to them and left for Macedonia. After traveling through that area and speaking many words of encouragement, he arrived in Greece, where he stayed three months. And when the Jews formed a plot against him as he was about to sail for Syria, he decided to go back through Macedonia.

Paul was accompanied by Sopater son of Pyrrhus from Berea, Aristarchus and Secundus from Thessalonica, Gaius from Derbe, Timothy, and Tychicus and Trophimus from the province of Asia. These men went on ahead and waited for us in Troas. And after the Feast of Unleavened Bread, we sailed from Philippi, and five days later we rejoined them in Troas, where we stayed seven days.

Commentary

There's not much in today's Scripture that needs discussion. It is simply a list of places visited and people who traveled with Paul. Paul sails to Macedonia (northern Greece) and then travels to southern Greece, or "Achaea." When he is about to leave Greece to return to Antioch by ship, some sort of plot against him by the Jews changes his plans, and he returns the way he came, via land to Macedonia. He catches a ship at Philippi.

Paul is at the geographical midpoint of his third journey; he has traveled from Antioch to (probably) Corinth and then turned around and headed home. In terms of time, however, it is late in his journey. He spent three years in Ephesus alone — from here he is headed pretty much straight home.

It is interesting to see how many men Paul has attracted as traveling companions. We continue to see the pronoun "we" used intermittently, most likely because Luke, like all of Paul's traveling companions, was sometimes with him and sometimes elsewhere.

Day 93 - Eutychus Raised from the Dead

Acts 20:7-12

On the first day of the week we came together to break bread. Since Paul was ready to leave the next day, he talked to them and kept on speaking until midnight.

Now there were many lamps in the upper room where we were gathered. And a certain young man named Eutychus, seated in the window, was sinking into a deep sleep as Paul talked on and on. When he was sound asleep, he fell from the third story and was picked up dead. But Paul went down, threw himself on the young man, and embraced him. "Do not be alarmed!" he said. "He is still alive!"

Then Paul went back upstairs, broke bread, and ate. And after speaking until daybreak, he departed. And the people were greatly relieved to take the boy home alive.

Commentary

If you have ever thought that your church services lasted a long time, this Scripture might change your mind. Paul's sermon starts at supper and runs until midnight. He was a world-class talker.

And his little congregation was only human; a long sermon, after supper, certainly put more than one listener to sleep. But Eutychus has the bad fortune to fall out a window from the third floor, thereby becoming immortalized in the Bible for going to sleep during a sermon. Luckily, he either did not die or was restored to life by Paul, so we can have a chuckle about it. Paul's sermon nearly bored one listener to death!

This story also reminds us of the sense of community that has been so diluted in much of the modern world, especially in larger cities. Before radio and television (and perhaps social media), when we were not bombarded with entertainment, people really did know their neighbors better. Modern technology is a wonderful thing, but there is a cost in terms of community. It is important to make an effort to know your neighbors better. We would all do well to make room in our schedule for community projects, weeknight church events, group Bible study, and other such joint activities.

"We should not stop gathering together with other believers, as some of you are doing. Instead, we must continue to encourage each other even more as we see the day of the Lord coming." (Hebrews 10:25)

Day 94 - In the Aegean Sea

Acts 20:13-16

We went on ahead to the ship and sailed to Assos, where we were to take Paul aboard. He had arranged this because he was going there on foot. And when he met us at Assos, we took him aboard and went on to Mitylene. Sailing on from there, we arrived the next day opposite Chios. The day after that we arrived at Samos, and on the following day we came to Miletus.

Paul had decided to sail past Ephesus to avoid spending time in the province of Asia, because he was in a hurry to reach Jerusalem, if possible, by the day of Pentecost.

Commentary

Today's verses are primarily just a travel diary. The first and last places mentioned, Assos and Miletus, were Greek seaside towns on the east coast of Anatolia; the other three are Greek islands (Mitylene is a town on the large island of Lesbos).

The narrator (probably Luke himself) is separated from Paul for a bit and recounts, for the first time, his own experience. It sounds as if the entire team, after so many years of hard work and danger, were ready to enjoy their cruise through the Greek Isles. I hope so. The route would have been as spectacular then as it is today.

We are left to guess why Paul wants to be in Jerusalem for Pentecost. There is no indication whether or not he intends a "Christian" holiday celebration; we are a long time before the calendar of Feast Days here.

Perhaps Paul partly wants to celebrate *Shavuot*. There is no prohibition against him participating in a Jewish holiday. Or perhaps, since *Shavuot* brings so many Jews into Jerusalem, he wants to have a crowd to preach to!

Day 95 - Paul's Farewell to the Ephesian Elders (1)

Acts 20:17-24

From Miletus, Paul sent to Ephesus for the elders of the church.

When they came to him, he said, "You know how I lived the whole time I was with you, from the first day I arrived in the province of Asia. I served the Lord with great humility and with tears, especially in the trials that came upon me through the plots of the Jews. I did not shrink back from declaring anything that was helpful to you as I taught you publicly and from house to house, testifying to Jews and Greeks alike about repentance to God and faith in our Lord Jesus Christ."

"And now, compelled by the Spirit, I am going to Jerusalem, not knowing what will happen to me there. I only know that in town after town the Holy Spirit warns me that chains and afflictions await me. But I consider my life of no value to me, if only I may finish my course and complete the ministry I have received from the Lord Jesus—the ministry of testifying to the good news of God's grace."

Commentary

Paul has called the elders of Ephesus to him for a goodbye speech. He has lived there for almost three years and, from all the circumstances, we can deduce that the Ephesus church has become important. We get some flavor of how he spent his time there: he preached in public, and he went from house to house. Now, he must go to Jerusalem, and it sounds ominous, parallel to Jesus returning to Jerusalem for trial and crucifixion.

The tone of this passage is consistent with other statements we have heard from Paul. He is never shy about telling how hard he has worked or what he has suffered. Still, he always adds that his work is meaningless except for the good he has done in spreading the word.

Paul is, in this sense, very much like anyone with significant achievements on earth. Pride is our nature. If we do work that appears great to other people, we will feel pride. We strive for humility, and we are blessed by the humility we find in life. But as humans, we do not achieve perfection. We must admit our failings and ask for forgiveness for pridefulness — and Paul is in the same boat.

Day 96 - Paul's Farewell to the Ephesian Elders (2)

Acts 20:25-31

Now I know that none of you among whom I have preached the kingdom will see my face again. Therefore I testify to you this day that I am innocent of the blood of all men. For I did not shrink back from declaring to you the whole will of God.

Keep watch over yourselves and the entire flock of which the Holy Spirit has made you overseers. Be shepherds of the church of God, which He purchased with His own blood. I know that after my departure, savage wolves will come in among you and will not spare the flock. Even from your own number, men will rise up and distort the truth to draw away disciples after them. Therefore be alert and remember that for three years I never stopped warning each of you night and day with tears.

Commentary

Paul's farewell is a heartfelt and emotional goodbye. They have lived together for so long that the feeling of community must have become intense. Paul, in his 50's by now, tells them he will not see them again. He is being led by the Holy Spirit to go to Jerusalem. It is a dangerous place for him. He anticipates trouble.

We cannot help but see a parallel to Jesus' long farewell in Ch. 14-17 of the *Gospel of John*. There are major differences: Paul does not have the certainty or destiny of being killed in Jerusalem, as Jesus did. Nor is his death nearly as significant. But Paul's primary ministry, spreading the Gospel and starting churches, is accomplished. He knows that it is time for him to move on, even if to his death.

We get an insight into how Paul converted people; he says that he warned them "with tears." Paul was a people person; his attempts to save souls involved complete direct contact with others, for however long it took, with great emotional involvement.

One of the warnings he gives is particularly appropriate to later times: "men will rise up and distort the truth to draw away disciples after them." Unfortunately, this phenomenon has plagued the church ever since. Men and women in every generation twist the Bible and gather followers, for their personal pride and worldly gain.

So, as Paul tells us: Be alert! The greatest protection we have for this is to read the Bible, to know the Bible, and to refuse to ignore the plain meaning of important passages. "Test everything" against the gospel Paul delivered to us. (1 Thessalonians 5:21)

Notice the phrase "innocent of the blood of all men." Paul implies that if he had not preached the gospel as forcefully as he had done, he would be guilty of their blood; this drives home the seriousness of Christ's final admonition to "go and make disciples of all nations" in Matthew 28:19.

We are reminded of his words in Acts 18:6 when he "shook out his garments" and told the Jews who opposed him, "Your blood be on your own heads! I am innocent of it."

The declaration echoes Ezekiel 3:18: "If I say to the wicked man, 'You will surely die,' but you do not warn him or speak out to warn him from his wicked way to save his life, that wicked man will die in his iniquity, and I will hold you responsible for his blood."

Day 97 - Paul's Farewell to the Ephesian Elders (3)

Acts 20:32-38

And now I commit you to God and to the word of His grace, which can build you up and give you an inheritance among all who are sanctified.

I have not coveted anyone's silver or gold or clothing. You yourselves know that these hands of mine have ministered to my own needs and those of my companions. In everything, I showed you that by this kind of hard work we must help the weak, remembering the words of the Lord Jesus Himself: 'It is more blessed to give than to receive.'"

When Paul had said this, he knelt down with all of them and prayed. They all wept openly as they embraced Paul and kissed him. They were especially grieved by his statement that they would never see his face again. Then they accompanied him to the ship.

Commentary

Paul gives himself as an example at the end of his farewell speech. But again, whatever we may think of Paul's pride, we cannot fault him for his sincerity. He has dedicated himself and his enormous talents — his mind, body, and soul— to the spread of Christ's word and grace. He was the instrument of God, in bringing Christianity to the world outside of Judea.

In this passage, Paul's admonitions to the elders concentrate on wealth, and he uses his own ministry as an example to be followed. He has spent only what was necessary to feed and clothe himself and his followers, and the source of his funds has been largely the work of his hands. (His financial faithfulness forms a stark contrast to some Christian leaders today . . . and even more to some Christian leaders in the Middle Ages!)

Paul's emphasis on "earning his keep" contrasts with his teachings that full-time Christian church leaders might be compensated. In 1 Corinthians 9:14 he wrote, "The Lord has commanded that those who preach the gospel should receive their living from the gospel." This verse suggests that churches should provide for the financial needs of their clergy.

Acts 21 – Paul Returns to Jerusalem

Day 98 - Paul Sets Sail for Home

Acts 21:1-7

After we had torn ourselves away from them, we sailed directly to Cos, and the next day on to Rhodes, and from there to Patara. Finding a ship crossing over to Phoenicia, we boarded it and set sail. After sighting Cyprus and passing south of it, we sailed on to Syria and landed at Tyre, where the ship was to unload its cargo.

We sought out the disciples in Tyre and stayed with them seven days. Through the Spirit they kept telling Paul not to go up to Jerusalem. But when our time there had ended, we set out on our journey. All the disciples, with their wives and children, accompanied us out of the city and knelt down on the beach to pray with us. And after we had said our farewells, we went aboard the ship, and they returned home.

When we had finished our voyage from Tyre, we landed at Ptolemais, where we greeted the brothers and stayed with them for a day.

Commentary

Once again, today's verses are mostly a travelogue, a first-person account of a ship voyage through the southeastern Greek Isles 2,000 years ago. After a couple of short hops on small coastal ships, Paul and his companions find a Phoenician freighter traveling all the way from Patara to Tyre, one of the great Phoenician trading ports, just north of the Hebrew colony of Galilee.

Paul is on the homeward leg of his "third journey." He and his companions left Antioch five years earlier and traveled the length of southern Anatolia, stopping to visit the little churches he founded on his second journey.

The first leg ended in Ephesus, where they built up a great church and remained for approximately three years, perhaps 54 A.D. to 57

A.D. From Ephesus, they ventured out into "Asia" to a number of un-named towns and villages.

Paul then more-or-less retraced his second journey through Macedonia and Achaia to visit and strengthen all the churches he had started there in his second journey; however, instead of sailing home from Greece, he circled back until he was just outside of Ephesus, to the smaller port of Miletus. There he summoned the elders of Ephesus and bid them farewell, and then sailed to Tyre. From Tyre, he will make his way by land to Jerusalem.

During his time in Ephesus and Corinth, Paul wrote what I would consider his most important epistles: *Galatians, 1 Corinthians, 2 Corinthians,* and *Romans.* These letters would come to lie at the heart of Christian theology, especially concerning his explication of salvation by grace.

Day 99 - Paul Visits Philip the Evangelist

Acts 21:8-14

Leaving the next day, we went on to Caesarea and stayed at the home of Philip the evangelist, who was one of the Seven. He had four unmarried daughters who prophesied.

After we had been there several days, a prophet named Agabus came down from Judea. Coming over to us, he took Paul's belt, bound his own feet and hands, and said, "The Holy Spirit says: 'In this way the Jews of Jerusalem will bind the owner of this belt and hand him over to the Gentiles.'" When we heard this, we and the people there pleaded with Paul not to go up to Jerusalem.

Then Paul answered, "Why are you weeping and breaking my heart? I am ready not only to be bound, but also to die in Jerusalem for the name of the Lord Jesus." When he would not be dissuaded, we fell silent and said, "The Lord's will be done."

Commentary

Paul previously landed in the Middle East at Tyre, from whence he has traveled south, down the coast to Ptolemais and now Caesarea, the capital of Roman Judea built by Herod the Great. It appears that he is still traveling by sea, but he will certainly proceed towards Jerusalem by land from this point.

We meet the remarkable Philip, once again: this is the Philip who was elected one of the seven deacons of Jerusalem (Acts 6:1-7) and later traveled to Samaria and Gaza, where he baptized an Ethiopian eunuch (Acts 8). There is no mention of why he had moved to Samaria, but he had shown an inclination to travel and baptize.

While in Philip's house, Paul receives a dramatic prophecy that he will be arrested in Jerusalem. He knows, however, that he is following in Christ's footsteps; so, like Christ, he is ready to be arrested and possibly executed when he arrives in Jerusalem.

Day 100 - Paul Goes to Jerusalem - Recap of Paul's Missionary Journeys

Acts 21:15-17

After these days, we packed up and went on to Jerusalem. Some of the disciples from Caesarea accompanied us, and they took us to stay at the home of Mnason the Cypriot, an early disciple.

When we arrived in Jerusalem, the brothers welcomed us joyfully.

Commentary

Paul's missionary journeys have ended. He will take an interesting fourth journey, but I would not call it a "missionary" journey, since it will not be strictly voluntary! (Spoiler alert: He will be sent to Rome in chains to stand trial.)

Also, he probably took a fifth journey to Spain, but we only know it from historical sources outside the Bible. We will discuss it in the final lesson.

So, let us briefly recap the three missionary journeys described in *Acts:*

All of them began in Paul's home base, Antioch. Paul's first journey, made with Barnabas, was relatively short. He sailed to Cyprus, then went north into the center of Anatolia. There he founded churches in a number of small towns and cities, after which he returned to Antioch. His route described a rough circle clockwise from Antioch.

The second lasted three years and was, really, the great missionary journey of Christianity. At the very start, Paul squabbled with Barnabas, who then made his own missionary journey to Cyprus; so Paul took Silas as his primary companion.

The second journey described a great circle, this time moving counterclockwise. Paul traveled the entire diagonal length of Anatolia from Antioch to the port of Troas, visiting the churches he founded in the first journey and starting new ones. (It was on this leg that he met Timothy.) He then crossed to northern Greece (Roman Macedonia) and traveled south to Corinth, starting churches all along the way.

From Corinth, he went to Athens for his remarkable encounter with the Greek philosophers. He then sailed home, stopping briefly at Ephesus.

The third and longest journey was largely similar in route to the second, with two differences. Instead of heading to Troas in northeastern Anatolia, Paul traveled west to Ephesus, where he spent roughly three years building up a major church in Ephesus itself. (Before Paul arrived, much of the church-building in Ephesus had been accomplished by the second-generation missionaries Aquila and Priscilla.)

He also traveled to unnamed small towns in the area around Ephesus (known to the Romans as "Asia"). He then visited the churches of Greece, but instead of taking a boat from Athens, he went back to the north of Greece by foot and then boated to Judea to make his way, ultimately, to Jerusalem.

These three journeys lasted approximately 12 years. He traveled 10,000 miles on primitive wooden ships and, by foot or donkey, over rough mountainous paths. He was hunted almost the entire time by furious Jewish authorities. He was seized and/or imprisoned countless times, badly beaten three times, and once, stoned and left for dead. And now, he returns to Jerusalem, where he knows he faces imprisonment and possibly execution.

So, let us take a second to remember this extraordinary man, who changed the course of history. If I ever think I have done "enough" for Christ, Paul's story sets me straight!

Day 101 - Paul Visits James in Jerusalem

Acts 21:18-26

The next day Paul went in with us to see James, and all the elders were present. Paul greeted them and recounted one by one the things that God had done among the Gentiles through his ministry.

When they heard this, they glorified God. Then they said to Paul, "You see, brother, how many thousands of Jews have believed, and all of them are zealous for the law. But they are under the impression that you teach all the Jews who live among the Gentiles to forsake Moses, telling them not to circumcise their children or observe our customs. What then should we do? They will certainly hear that you have come.

Therefore do what we advise you. There are four men with us who have taken a vow. Take these men, purify yourself along with them, and pay their expenses so they can have their heads shaved. Then everyone will know that there is no truth to these rumors about you, but that you also live in obedience to the law.

As for the Gentile believers, we have written to them our decision that they must abstain from food sacrificed to idols, from blood, from the meat of strangled animals, and from sexual immorality."

So the next day Paul took the men and purified himself along with them. Then he entered the temple to give notice of the date when their purification would be complete and the offering would be made for each of them.

Commentary

Paul arrives in Jerusalem and goes immediately to see James the Just, who was the first bishop of Jerusalem and the author of the *Epistle of James*. Most Protestant scholars believe he was Jesus' natural half-brother, while Catholic scholars teach that he was a cousin.

The thriving church in Jerusalem was composed almost entirely of Jews, but there is no mention of persecution. Apparently, Jerusalem's Jewish authorities had learned that the new Jesus sect had no political ambitions and allowed it to exist in some degree of peace.

Paul was another matter. He had irked many people. The mixing of Gentile and Jewish Christians, uncommon in Jerusalem, was widespread in the Pauline churches of Greece. Thus, Jerusalem was vulnerable to rumors and lies about these distant churches.

Whether maliciously or simply by mistake, word had spread that Paul's Jewish converts had completely abandoned Judaism. James, therefore, advises Paul to underwrite a Jewish purification ritual for four men who had taken a vow, and also to undergo the ritual himself, to show that he continues to honor the laws of Moses. (In fact, Paul himself had "taken the vow"—a Nazirite vow, similar to the one that Samson had lived under — while on his second journey.)

It isn't going to work, though; as we will see next, Paul is and will remain a *persona* very much *non grata* in Jerusalem!

Day 102 - Paul Attacked in the Temple

Acts 21:27-30

When the seven days were almost over, some Jews from the province of Asia saw Paul at the temple. They stirred up the whole crowd and seized him, crying out, "Men of Israel, help us! This is the man who teaches everywhere against our people and against our law and against this place. Furthermore, he has brought Greeks into the temple and defiled this holy place." For they had previously seen Trophimus the Ephesian with him in the city, and they assumed that Paul had brought him into the temple.

The whole city was stirred up, and the people rushed together. They seized Paul and dragged him out of the temple, and at once the gates were shut.

Commentary

Paul had not been in Jerusalem (or even in Judea) for over twenty years. But he made enemies on his travels, some of whom have come to Jerusalem and recognize him.

To scotch a rumor that he had become anti-Jewish, Paul undertook sponsorship of Nazirite purification for four men, something that only a devout Jew would do.

Of course, the rumors were false. Even today, many Christians follow Jewish observances from time to time. Some churches, such as the Seventh-day Adventists (who keep the Jewish Sabbath), retain Jewish customs, and many Christians celebrate Passover and even hold modified Seder services.

So Paul demonstrates, in effect, that Christ did not come to abolish the law. (*See* Matthew 5:17-20.) But it is futile. The Nazirite purification is a seven-day process, time enough for his enemies to hear that Paul is in the Temple. They incite a crowd against him by spreading a falsehood that Paul is bringing Gentiles into the Temple, and the angry mob drags him away!

Paul's attempt to build bridges between the Jews and Christ is to no avail. Wherever he has gone, intransigent Jews have erupted against him; and now he is in the very heart of Judaism, and his enemies have him in their clutches.

Day 103 - Paul Saved from the Mob and Arrested

Acts 21:31-36

While they were trying to kill him, the commander of the Roman regiment received a report that all Jerusalem was in turmoil. Immediately he took some soldiers and centurions and ran down to the crowd. When the people saw the commander and the soldiers, they stopped beating Paul.

The commander came up and arrested Paul, ordering that he be bound with two chains. Then he asked who he was and what he had done.

Some in the crowd were shouting one thing, and some another. And since the commander could not get at the truth because of the uproar, he ordered that Paul be brought into the barracks. When Paul reached the steps, he had to be carried by the soldiers because of the violence of the mob. For the crowd that followed him kept shouting, "Away with him!"

Commentary

Although there were many evils in the Roman Empire, it did keep "law and order" in its colonies, at a time when the world was often lawless and chaotic. As horrible by today's standards as Roman rule might have been, the *pax romana* (the historical "Roman peace," which allowed Paul to travel in relative safety around the Mediterranean) would be remembered fondly in the Dark Ages to follow.

We see it operating in today's lesson. The Roman commander in Jerusalem will not allow mob violence and thus saves Paul's life. But arrest by Roman soldiers is hardly a guarantee of safety, is it? Paul, like Jesus, will still face trial.

But Jesus was condemned by the Sanhedrin, the ruling body of Judaism; Paul is simply the target of a mob. Also, the Roman governor will treat Paul much differently than Jesus, because Paul is a Roman citizen and Jesus was not.

Also like Jesus, Paul has traveled to Jerusalem knowing that he will be arrested. As we saw earlier in Acts 21:10, a man named Agabus dramatically prophesied that Paul would be arrested and turned over to the Romans.

The entire tone of the passage is ominous. One gets the feeling from *Acts* that Paul's return to Jerusalem, after an absence of 30 years, is some sort of bookend to his ministry. He has explicitly speculated that he is coming to the end of his journey.

Finally, there will be one enormous difference between the trials of Paul and Jesus. Paul will defend himself, and his defense will succeed—he will not be crucified in Jerusalem.

Day 104 - Paul Defends Himself to the Crowd in Jerusalem (1)

Acts 21:37-40

As they were about to take Paul into the barracks, he asked the commander, "May I say something to you?"

"Do you speak Greek?" he replied. "Aren't you the Egyptian who incited a rebellion some time ago and led four thousand members of the Assassins into the wilderness?"

But Paul answered, "I am a Jew from Tarsus in Cilicia, a citizen of no ordinary city. Now I beg you to allow me to speak to the people."

Having received permission, Paul stood on the steps and motioned to the crowd. A great hush came over the crowd, and he addressed them in Hebrew:

Commentary

The ignorance of the commander is so startling it is humorous. Not only does he think Paul is Egyptian, but he thinks he led 4,000 people into the wilderness. Is he confusing Paul with Moses? The reference is obscure; there might have been an unrecorded uprising coming from Egypt in the recent past, and the reference to "Assassins" probably refers to the *Sicarii*, a sect of violent Hebrew zealots sworn to defeating the Romans.

Then we discover that the crowd is similarly ignorant, for they are surprised to hear Paul speaking Hebrew.

We, as Christians, face similar problems of ignorance, confusion, and hysteria today. The ignorance (and even intentional untruthfulness) of non-Christians with respect to Biblical teaching can be astonishing.

People are driven away from Christ, and become less willing to hear the Gospel, when their ears are saturated by anti-Christian news. And who can blame them? Propaganda is effective, and anti-Christian propaganda, even if it is utterly false, can sway the opinion of the ignorant. And all too often, news about evil acts of Christians, even Christian leaders, is true!

But when they know the truth, they are like the commander and crowd when they hear Paul speak. Simply knowing that Paul speaks Hebrew quiets the crowd down. Truth defeats mob ignorance.

Christ told us, "Let your light shine before others, so that they may see your good works and glorify your Father who is in heaven." (Matthew 5:16) We are responsible for telling the world about true Christian belief and the good works that have been done in Christ's name. This very day, untold charitable works are being done by Christians all over the world. We must not shrink from promoting the faith; it is not bragging. It is something that Christ himself instructed us to do.

In words formerly attributed to St. Francis of Assisi, "Preach the Gospel at all times; if necessary, use words."

Bonus Material: Languages in First Century Judea

There were four primary languages in Judea: Latin, Greek, Aramaic, and Hebrew. The native language of the region was Aramaic, a Semitic language spoken over much of the Middle East. Many references to "the language of the Hebrews" or even "Hebrew" mean Aramaic. This is the language Jesus and Paul primarily spoke.

The second most widely spoken language was Greek. It was actually the common language of the Roman Empire. Paul would have spoken fluent Greek as that was the language, not only of the Gentiles, but also of the Jews in Ephesus, Corinth, etc.

Latin was spoken pretty much only by Romans.

Some Jewish scholars claim that Hebrew was still widely spoken, but more likely, it was limited to religious usage, i.e. in the synagogues.

Acts 22 – Paul on Trial in Jerusalem

Day 105 - Paul Defends Himself to the Crowd in Jerusalem (2)

Acts 22:1-16

"Brothers and fathers, listen now to my defense before you." When they heard him speak to them in Hebrew, they became even more silent.

Then Paul declared, "I am a Jew, born in Tarsus of Cilicia, but raised in this city. I was educated at the feet of Gamaliel in strict conformity to the law of our fathers. I was just as zealous for God as any of you are today.

I persecuted this Way even to the death, detaining both men and women and throwing them into prison, as the high priest and the whole Council can testify about me. I even obtained letters from them to their brothers in Damascus, and I was on my way to apprehend these people and bring them to Jerusalem to be punished.

About noon as I was approaching Damascus, suddenly a bright light from heaven flashed around me. I fell to the ground and heard a voice say to me, 'Saul, Saul, why do you persecute Me?'

'Who are You, Lord?' I asked.

'I am Jesus of Nazareth, whom you are persecuting,' He replied. My companions saw the light, but they could not understand the voice of the One speaking to me.

Then I asked, 'What should I do, Lord?'

'Get up and go into Damascus,' He told me. 'There you will be told all that you have been appointed to do.'

Because the brilliance of the light had blinded me, my companions led me by the hand into Damascus. There a man named Ananias, a devout observer of the law who was highly regarded by all the Jews living there, came and stood beside me. 'Brother Saul,' he said, 'receive your sight.' And at that moment I could see him.

Then he said, 'The God of our fathers has appointed you to know His will and to see the Righteous One and to hear His voice. You will be His witness to everyone of what you have seen and heard. And now what are you waiting for? Get up, be baptized, and wash your sins away, calling on His name.'

Commentary

If you think that Paul's "defense" is not very likely to placate the mob for long, you're right. Instead of appeasing them by telling them that he is a good Jew, he is actually leading up to telling them why their brand of Judaism is no longer valid.

Paul tells the crowd his actual, truthful story. And, at the same time, he manages to deliver the Gospel of Christ to the crowd.

He has a large and attentive audience, and he isn't going to waste the opportunity, even if it is his last!

Day 106 - Paul Defends Himself to the Crowd in Jerusalem (3)

Acts 22:17-21

"Later, when I had returned to Jerusalem and was praying at the temple, I fell into a trance and saw the Lord saying to me, 'Hurry! Leave Jerusalem quickly, because the people here will not accept your testimony about Me.'

'Lord,' I answered, 'they know very well that in one synagogue after another I imprisoned and beat those who believed in You. And when the blood of Your witness Stephen was shed, I stood there giving my approval and watching over the garments of those who killed him.'

Then He said to me, 'Go! I will send you far away to the Gentiles.'"

Commentary

Today's Scripture is the last part of Paul's "defense" to the crowd in Jerusalem.

As we suspected in the earlier verses, Paul is not really defending himself; his speech is not intended to pacify the mob. He is, rather, preaching the gospel, and we know from the reactions of mobs in his earlier journeys that preaching the gospel leads to violence. In the eyes of those who will not accept Christ, his speech constitutes an admission that he is subverting Judaism.

On a side note, while much of Paul's speech is a rehash of Acts 9, he adds new information. His mission to the Gentiles was given to him the first time he came to Jerusalem after his conversion, not in Antioch. It was the fulfillment of God's ancient promise, to bring His Messiah to the Gentiles. *(E.g.* Isaiah 49:6, "I will make you a light to the nations, that my salvation may reach to the ends of the earth.")

So now we see the big picture, a fifteen or twenty-year journey beginning and ending in Jerusalem. Paul has followed his orders. He has traveled huge distances by land and sea, founding and overseeing churches throughout the Greek world. Mission accomplished!

Day 107 - Paul's Roman Citizenship

Acts 22:22-29

The crowd listened to Paul until he made this statement. Then they lifted up their voices and shouted, "Rid the earth of him! He is not fit to live!"

As they were shouting and throwing off their cloaks and tossing dust into the air, the commander ordered that Paul be brought into the barracks. He directed that Paul be flogged and interrogated to determine the reason for this outcry against him.

But as they stretched him out to strap him down, Paul said to the centurion standing there, "Is it lawful for you to flog a Roman citizen without a trial?"

On hearing this, the centurion went and reported it to the commander. "What are you going to do?" he said. "This man is a Roman citizen."

The commander went to Paul and asked, "Tell me, are you a Roman citizen?"

"Yes," he answered.

"I paid a high price for my citizenship," said the commander.

"But I was born a citizen," Paul replied.

At once those who were about to interrogate Paul stepped back, and the commander himself was alarmed when he realized that he had put a Roman citizen in chains.

Commentary

Paul had quieted down the crowd by speaking in Hebrew (or Aramaic). But as soon as he uses the word "Gentiles," they erupt again. Any admission of consorting with Gentiles is enough to enrage a Jewish lynch mob.

The Roman cohort holds the mob at bay, taking Paul into the comparative safety of the barracks. Here, we get an interesting insight into Roman legal procedure. The centurion assumes Paul is just some conquered colonial, so he plans to simply "beat the truth out of him."

But binding and scourging a <u>citizen</u> without due cause are not allowed under Roman law. Just as in every colonized land in history, Romans are treated differently than the colonized peoples.

Acts 23 – The Plot to Kill Paul

Day 108 - Paul Before the Sanhedrin (1)

Acts 22:30, 23:1-5

The next day the commander, wanting to learn the real reason Paul was accused by the Jews, released him and ordered the chief priests and the whole Sanhedrin to assemble. Then he brought Paul down and had him stand before them.

Paul looked directly at the Sanhedrin and said, "Brothers, I have conducted myself before God in all good conscience to this day."

At this, the high priest Ananias ordered those standing near Paul to strike him on the mouth.

Then Paul said to him, "God will strike you, you whitewashed wall! You sit here to judge me according to the law, yet you yourself violate the law by commanding that I be struck."

But those standing nearby said, "How dare you insult the high priest of God!"

"Brothers," Paul replied, "I was not aware that he was the high priest, for it is written: 'Do not speak evil about the ruler of your people.'"

Commentary Part I

We meet a new and particularly nasty character here, High Priest Ananias ben Nedebeus (Ananias, the son of Nedebeus), who overcame the dynastic line of Annas to become high priest from 46-59 A.D. Do not confuse him with the great Ananias of Damascus, the man who baptized Paul (and the person usually meant when the simple name "Ananias" is used).

Ananias ben Nedebeus was a corrupt, greedy, and hypocritical man, an unscrupulous politician who held his post by collaborating with the

Romans. He was well-known for his brutality; so when he had a guard hit Paul in the mouth, for nothing more than claiming to live in good conscience before God, it would not have surprised anyone.

Paul calls him a "whitewashed wall." It is an odd-sounding insult to us, but consider when we talk about somebody in power covering up wrongdoing, we call it a "whitewash." (Jesus, Job, and Ezekiel all used the same expression. See, *e.g.*, Ezekiel 13:11-15.) This is just how Paul means it. Ananias ben Nedebeus is an entire wall of whitewash, a person who covers a mass of hypocrisy with a thin veneer of respectability.

And what does Paul do? He apologizes! Paul retracts his insult, not because it is untrue, but because the Bible forbids it. (*E.g.* Exodus 22:28.) Paul had not realized Ananias was the high priest.

Every religion, at some point in its history, seems to have encountered men like Ananias ben Nedebeus: dynamic men of little actual faith or integrity, but having enormous political intelligence, who use their talents to become a religious leader for the sole purpose of gaining power and wealth. It is the way of this world.

Ananias ben Nedebeus did not get away with his hypocrisy forever. The governor of Syria had him arrested and sent to Rome for excessive brutality. Although the emperor (Claudius) acquitted him, it did him no good; when he returned to Jerusalem, he was hunted down and murdered by Jewish nationalists.

Commentary Part II – Staying Out of Politics

Although the history is interesting, it is a minor subject compared to the primary message of the passage. There is a direct commandment in the passage that a great majority of Christians simply ignore.

Paul demonstrates, for our benefit, that the Old Testament commandment — "You must not speak evil of a ruler of your people" — is still in full force and effect. Whatever we might think of the Old Testament, Paul's apology reiterates the commandment as a law directly and clearly binding on Christians.

If we speak evil of the president (prime minister, governor, etc.) we disobey God and destroy Christian unity, no matter how much we might disagree with the person's politics.

This is one of those New Testament maxims that people hate to obey; but it is the word of God. I have heard countless arguments, from liberals and conservatives alike, that the current government is evil and their candidate is more Christian and should be elected.

We are welcome to our opinions. But where they conflict with a clear and direct Biblical command, we need to stop talking and start listening.

Moreover, the injunction stated here is, first, directly in the context of criticizing a corrupt ruler, and second, consistent with the entirety of the New Testament. Romans 13 tells us, for example, "Everyone must submit himself to the governing authorities, for there is no authority except that which God has established."

Politics is earthly power. If we look at the life of Christ, what do we see? A constant refusal to engage in secular politics. "Render unto Caesar that which is Caesar's." I have scoured the Bible looking for a statement from Christ to take over the civil government, and it is not there. In John 6:15, we see Him leaving a crowd to prevent them from making him their king.

Service to politics is service to earthly power, and love of political power excludes love for Christ. "No man can serve two masters: for either he will hate the one, and love the other; or else he will hold to the one, and despise the other, Ye cannot serve God and mammon." (Matthew 6:24)

Day 109 - Paul Before the Sanhedrin (2)

Acts 23:6-10

Then Paul, knowing that some of them were Sadducees and the others Pharisees, called out in the Sanhedrin, "Brothers, I am a Pharisee, the son of a Pharisee. It is because of my hope in the resurrection of the dead that I am on trial."

As soon as he had said this, a dispute broke out between the Pharisees and Sadducees, and the assembly was divided. For the Sadducees say that there is neither a resurrection nor angels nor spirits, but the Pharisees acknowledge them all.

A great clamor arose, and some scribes from the party of the Pharisees got up and contended sharply, "We find nothing wrong with this man. What if a spirit or an angel has spoken to him?" The dispute grew so violent that the commander was afraid they would tear Paul to pieces. He ordered the soldiers to go down and remove him by force and bring him into the barracks.

Commentary

The Sadducees were the conservative sect that we would associate with ancient Hebrews. Theirs was a Judaism dominated by priests, emphasizing the sacrifice of animals. The Pharisees, dominated by teachers, were the sect that we would recognize as modern Judaism. They believed in heaven and hell, taught some degree of pre-Christian forgiveness, and were attuned to reading and learning.

Oddly, the conservative Sadducees tended to be stronger in urban areas, probably because they were so aligned with the Temple of Jerusalem. Many of the high priests were Sadducees.

Paul was always clever about handling men. He was a master orator, a skilled debater, and he certainly understood divisiveness. Here, finding himself in trouble with the high priest Ananias ben Nedebeus, he instantly realizes how he can keep from being condemned and punished by the Sanhedrin: get them arguing among themselves.

He doesn't lie about his belief in Christ; he simply doesn't choose to volunteer the information at this specific time. The Sanhedrin knows almost nothing about him since his ministry has been far from Judea, and when he states his sympathy with the Pharisees and says that he is being persecuted for his belief in the resurrection of the dead—which is technically true—the Pharisees jump to his defense.

And so, the Roman commander, who has just rescued Paul from a disruptive mob, must now rescue him from a disruptive Sanhedrin.

Day 110 - The Plot to Kill Paul (1)

Acts 23:11-16

The following night the Lord stood near Paul and said, "Take courage! As you have testified about Me in Jerusalem, so also you must testify in Rome."

When daylight came, the Jews formed a conspiracy and bound themselves with an oath not to eat or drink until they had killed Paul. More than forty of them were involved in this plot. They went to the chief priests and elders and said, "We have bound ourselves with a solemn oath not to eat anything until we have killed Paul. Now then, you and the Sanhedrin petition the commander to bring him down to you on the pretext of examining his case more carefully. We are ready to kill him on the way."

But when the son of Paul's sister heard about the plot, he went into the barracks and told Paul.

Commentary

History is replete with groups of men forming sworn cabals to murder a prominent person. (In fact, only a few years earlier, a similar small group of senators had assassinated the horrific Caligula in Rome.)

This group of Sadducees is almost certainly in league with the chief high priest, Ananias ben Nedebeus, who was known for his nefarious and brutal tactics. They have two reasons to murder Paul. First, his Christian preaching; and now, he has joined with the Pharisees against the Sadducees, by arguing for resurrection after death.

Paul's nephew, whom we have not met before, seems to have inherited his uncle's wits. He somehow discovers the plot and immediately tells Paul.

Day 111 - The Plot to Kill Paul (2)

Acts 23:17-35

Then Paul called one of the centurions and said, "Take this young man to the commander; he has something to tell him."

So the centurion took him to the commander and said, "Paul the prisoner sent and asked me to bring this young man to you. He has something to tell you."

The commander took the young man by the hand, drew him aside, and asked, "What do you need to tell me?"

He answered, "The Jews have agreed to ask you to bring Paul to the Sanhedrin tomorrow on the pretext of acquiring more information about him. Do not let them persuade you, because more than forty men are waiting to ambush him. They have bound themselves with an oath not to eat or drink until they have killed him; they are ready now, awaiting your consent."

So the commander dismissed the young man and instructed him, "Do not tell anyone that you have reported this to me."

Then he called two of his centurions and said, "Prepare two hundred soldiers, seventy horsemen, and two hundred spearmen to go to Caesarea in the third hour of the night. Provide mounts for Paul to take him safely to Governor Felix."

And he wrote the following letter:

Claudius Lysias,

To His Excellency, Governor Felix:

Greetings.

This man was seized by the Jews, and they were about to kill him when I came with my troops to rescue him. For I had learned that he is a Roman citizen, and since I wanted to understand their charges against him, I brought him down to their Sanhedrin. I found that the accusation involved questions about their own law, but there was no charge worthy of death or imprisonment.

When I was informed that there was a plot against the man, I sent him to you at once. I also instructed his accusers to present their case against him before you.

So the soldiers followed their orders and brought Paul by night to Antipatris. The next day they returned to the barracks and let the horsemen go on with him. When the horsemen arrived in Caesarea, they delivered the letter to the governor and presented Paul to him.

The governor read the letter and asked what province Paul was from. Learning that he was from Cilicia, he said, "I will hear your case when your accusers arrive." Then he ordered that Paul be kept under guard in Herod's Praetorium.

Commentary

Today's Scripture is a straightforward account of the commander of the Jerusalem garrison removing Paul, a Roman citizen, from the danger of being killed by a colonial mob. He sends Paul under guard to the comparative safety of Caesarea, the capital of Roman Judea.

Do not think that Roman law had anything resembling the fair-mindedness or dedication to justice that one associates with the American legal system. The protection of Paul was rooted in politics. The Roman commander (Claudius Lysias) and the governor (Felix) have only a modicum of interest in treating Paul fairly. Their first concern is Roman dignity. Even though Ananias ben Nedebeus is the highest-ranking Jewish leader, the Jews are a conquered and subjugated nation; Paul is a Roman citizen. The Romans simply would not allow one of their citizens to be tried and punished by a Jewish court.

Notice how different this is from the trial and crucifixion of Jesus. There, Pontius Pilate, who seemed reasonably fair-minded, considered Jesus to be innocent; nevertheless, Jesus had no status in Roman eyes. So Pilate was willing to let the Sanhedrin convict Him as they saw fit and even carried out the execution for them.

Acts 24 – Paul Tried by Felix

Day 112 - Felix Hears the Charges Against Paul, at Caesarea

Acts 24:1-9

Five days later the high priest Ananias came down with some elders and a lawyer named Tertullus, who presented to the governor their case against Paul.

When Paul had been called in, Tertullus opened the prosecution: "Because of you, we have enjoyed a lasting peace, and your foresight has brought improvements to this nation. In every way and everywhere, most excellent Felix, we acknowledge this with all gratitude. But in order not to delay you any further, I beg your indulgence to hear us briefly.

We have found this man to be a pestilence, stirring up dissension among the Jews all over the world. He is a ringleader of the sect of the Nazarenes, and he even tried to desecrate the temple; so we seized him. By examining him yourself, you will be able to learn the truth about all our charges against him."

The Jews concurred, asserting that these charges were true.

Commentary

Having failed in their plot to murder Paul in Jerusalem, Ananias ben Nedebeus and his toadies must travel to Caesarea; rather than sitting as the judges in the case, they have been reduced to petitioners before the Roman court.

It is not clear why Tertullus presents the case rather than Ananias. Perhaps Ananias is too proud to appear as a petitioner before another court, acknowledging his subordination to Felix. Perhaps Tertullus is a powerful orator, or can speak in Latin, or understands the Roman laws. Perhaps Tertullus knows Felix.

At any rate, Tertullus acts like a modern-day attorney; he presents a well-conceived argument. He speaks of the beneficial peace in Judea and then paints Paul as a person who would destroy that peace. The first accusation he makes is that Paul stirs up riots among Jews, not only in Judea but "in all the world," i.e. throughout the Roman empire.

This is the charge that will get Rome's full attention. The Jews chafed under Roman rule. (And, in fact, eight years later, the Jews would start a full-fledged rebellion, the First Jewish-Roman War, that would last for seven years.) Felix's first order of business, as governor of Judea, is to prevent riots which might lead to rebellion.

Tertullus' second accusation, presented more as a matter of explanation, was that Paul is a leader of the heretical Nazarene Sect, i.e. Christianity. This was of enormous importance to the Sanhedrin. It had some minor importance to Felix, also, since he wanted to curry favor with whichever sect held power over the Jews.

An important ulterior motive of the Jews, however, is not even mentioned to the Roman court. Paul had avoided condemnation in the Sanhedrin by identifying his beliefs with those of the Pharisees; so Ananias ben Nedebeus has a hidden agenda to diminish Pharisee influence.

Day 113 - Paul's Defense to Felix

Acts 24:10-21

When the governor motioned for Paul to speak, he began his response: "Knowing that you have been a judge over this nation for many years, I gladly make my defense. You can verify for yourself that no more than twelve days ago I went up to Jerusalem to worship. Yet my accusers did not find me debating with anyone in the temple or riling up a crowd in the synagogues or in the city. Nor can they prove to you any of their charges against me.

I do confess to you, however, that I worship the God of our fathers according to the Way, which they call a sect. I believe everything that is laid down by the Law and written in the Prophets, and I have the same hope in God that they themselves cherish, that there will be a resurrection of both the righteous and the wicked. In this hope, I strive always to maintain a clear conscience before God and man.

After several years, then, I returned to Jerusalem to bring alms to my people and to present offerings. At the time they found me in the temple, I was ceremonially clean and was not inciting a crowd or an uproar. But there are some Jews from the province of Asia who ought to appear before you and bring charges, if they have anything against me. Otherwise, let these men state for themselves any crime they found in me when I stood before the Sanhedrin, unless it was this one thing I called out as I stood in their presence: 'It is concerning the resurrection of the dead that I am on trial before you today.'"

Commentary

Paul makes his defense before the Roman governor Felix, in Caesarea, the capital of Roman Judea. Paul has been accused of trying to profane the high temple and of stirring up Jews to riot throughout the empire as the leader of the "Nazarene sect."

Paul is wholly innocent of trying to profane the temple. In fact, while he was in Jerusalem, he spent much of his time at the temple performing a traditional Jewish purification ritual; and, uncharacteristically, he did not preach.

As to the second charge, Paul does not even claim to be innocent. None of the Jews from "Asia" (the area around Ephesus in northwestern Anatolia), however, have come to Caesarea to testify. There are no witnesses against him. His defense is, essentially, that he is innocent until proven guilty, and they have no proof.

The one thing that they can prove is that he caused a disruption in the Sanhedrin itself. During his trial in the Sanhedrin, he divided the council against itself, by claiming he was being persecuted for preaching the resurrection of the dead. This inflamed the Pharisee council members (who believe in the resurrection of the dead and spirits) against the Sadducees (who do not).

But it is impossible for the governor, Felix, to condemn Paul on this point. The Pharisees are a powerful Jewish sect; to find a man guilty of wrongdoing, for preaching the Pharisee doctrine of resurrection, would invite civil war among the Jews, and possibly rebellion against Rome.

Day 114 - Paul Kept in Custody

Acts 24:22-27

Then Felix, who was well informed about the Way, adjourned the hearing and said, "When Lysias the commander comes, I will decide your case." He ordered the centurion to keep Paul under guard, but to allow him some freedom and permit his friends to minister to his needs.

After several days, Felix returned with his wife Drusilla, who was a Jewess. He sent for Paul and listened to him speak about faith in Christ Jesus. As Paul expounded on righteousness, self-control, and the coming judgment, Felix became frightened and said, "You may go for now. When I find the time, I will call for you." At the same time, he was hoping that Paul would offer him a bribe. So he sent for Paul frequently and talked with him.

After two years had passed, Felix was succeeded by Porcius Festus. And wishing to do the Jews a favor, Felix left Paul in prison.

Commentary

Felix was an interesting character in his own right. He had been a Greek slave of Emperor Claudius (or possibly Claudius' wife. He was freed and rose quickly in status and wealth; unfortunately, his rise was fueled by corruption and his lack of scruples as much as by intelligence. He was not a well-regarded governor. He seemed better at acquiring power than exercising it.

His treatment of Paul shows his character. Although he is not gratuitously cruel to Paul — he does not convict him falsely and allows him some freedom and comforts while in custody — neither does he find Paul innocent of the charges and set him free, as the evidence would demand. Instead, he waits for a bribe; and not getting one, he lets Paul rot for two years, so as not to upset Ananias ben Nedebeus and the Sanhedrin without receiving a tangible reward.

The account of Felix's private audience with Paul is amusing. Paul tells Felix about salvation through Christ and the hell that awaits those who do not repent. Felix neither accepts nor rejects Paul's doctrine. Instead, he "becomes alarmed" at the thought that God's judgment awaits his conduct, for he is too attached to his corruption to repent. Like any hypocrite, Felix is more upset with someone exposing his wickedness than about the wickedness itself.

After a while, though, his curiosity and intelligence begin to show. Like Pontius Pilate with Jesus, Felix is fascinated by Paul. Pilate and Felix resemble a great many people today, those who put one toe into Christianity and perhaps even attend church on occasion, but simply cannot bear to give up their attachment to the visible world, and so are lost.

After the events of this passage, Felix was recalled to Rome to stand trial for corruption. He was saved by the emperor's intervention, but his public career was finished.

Acts 25 – Paul's Defense to Festus

Day 115 - Festus Hears Charges Against Paul

Acts 25:1-7

Three days after his arrival in the province, Festus went up from Caesarea to Jerusalem, where the chief priests and Jewish leaders presented their case against Paul. They urged Festus to grant them a concession against Paul by summoning him to Jerusalem, because they were preparing an ambush to kill him along the way.

But Festus replied, "Paul is being held in Caesarea, and I myself am going there soon. So if this man has done anything wrong, let some of your leaders come down with me and accuse him there."

After spending no more than eight or ten days with them, Festus went down to Caesarea. The next day he sat on the judgment seat and ordered that Paul be brought in. When Paul arrived, the Jews who had come down from Jerusalem stood around him, bringing many serious charges that they could not prove.

Commentary

Festus is Porcius Festus, the new procurator (governor) of Galilee and Judea. When he arrives, Paul has been under arrest in Caesarea for over two years; Festus' predecessor (Felix) handled the difficult situation by simply doing nothing. The Jewish authorities in the Sanhedrin were quiet as long as Paul was held in prison, and Felix would not find him innocent without a bribe. On the other hand, there was no evidence of Paul's guilt, and Felix would not find him guilty.

Festus is faced with the same situation as Felix had been. The Jews want Paul transferred to Jerusalem so that they can murder him. And once again, a trial is held, just as it had been two years before.

Festus was, by all accounts, a fair-minded and honest governor, in stark contrast to his predecessor, but he did not have Felix's experience and knowledge. He especially did not have Felix's deep knowledge of Judaism; Felix, after all, was married to a Jew. Also, the Sanhedrin certainly had a part in Felix's recall to Rome, so Festus would not have wanted to offend them unnecessarily.

The *Book of Acts* skips over the details of the charges against Paul, Paul's defense, and the Jewish authorities involved. (Ananias ben Nedebeus had, by this time, been replaced as high priest.) We will find out more details later in Chapter 25, however, when Festus discusses the case with Agrippa (the current Jewish king) and his sister Bernice.

Day 116 - Paul Demands an Appeal to Caesar

Acts 25:8-12

Then Paul made his defense: "I have committed no offense against the law of the Jews or against the temple or against Caesar."

But Festus, wishing to do the Jews a favor, said to Paul, "Are you willing to go up to Jerusalem to stand trial before me on these charges?"

Paul replied, "I am standing before the judgment seat of Caesar, where I ought to be tried. I have done nothing wrong to the Jews, as you yourself know very well. If, however, I am guilty of anything worthy of death, I do not refuse to die. But if there is no truth to their accusations against me, no one has the right to hand me over to them. I appeal to Caesar!"

Then Festus conferred with his council and replied, "You have appealed to Caesar. To Caesar you will go!"

Commentary

The short description of Paul's defense tells us, by implication, the general charges that had been brought against him. We also know from his first trial that the prosecutors have no evidence to support any of the claims. Clearly, he has not committed any offense against Caesar — Festus would have found him guilty of any proven offense against Roman law, and the Jews' complaints would have become a moot point.

The Jews convince the inexperienced Festus that he should move the trial to Jerusalem, a more appropriate venue for the charges of offenses against Jewish law and the temple. But, as we know, the Jews have no intention of allowing Paul another trial; they intend to murder him.

So Paul, who has no intention of being murdered by the Jewish authorities, throws a monkey wrench into the works. As a Roman citizen living in a colony, Paul has a right to demand an appeal to the Emperor of Rome. He cannot be tried by a local court, such as the Sanhedrin, against his will. And Festus has no choice but to grant the appeal.

Day 117 - Agrippa and Bernice

Acts 25:13-22

After several days had passed, King Agrippa and Bernice came down to Caesarea to pay their respects to Festus. Since they were staying several days, Festus laid out Paul's case before the king: "There is a certain man whom Felix left in prison. While I was in Jerusalem, the chief priests and elders of the Jews presented their case and requested a judgment against him. I told them that it is not the Roman custom to hand a man over before he has had an opportunity to face his accusers and defend himself against their charges.

So when they came here with me, I did not delay. The next day I sat on the judgment seat and ordered that the man be brought in. But when his accusers rose to speak, they did not charge him with any of the crimes I had expected. They only had some contentions with him regarding their own religion and a certain Jesus who had died, but whom Paul affirmed to be alive.

Since I was at a loss as to how to investigate these matters, I asked if he was willing to go to Jerusalem and be tried there on these charges. But when Paul appealed to be held over for the decision of the Emperor, I ordered that he be held until I could send him to Caesar."

Then Agrippa said to Festus, "I would like to hear this man myself."

"Tomorrow you will hear him," Festus declared.

Commentary

Much of *Acts* touches on the history of the Middle East, and today we encounter two new figures, Agrippa and Bernice. I hate to say this, but Agrippa is yet another Herod, "Herod Agrippa II," the son of Herod Agrippa I. Fortunately, the son whom we encounter today is known simply as Agrippa. He was the last king of the Herod dynasty.

Bernice, Agrippa's sister, had an interesting life. She reigned as a client queen of Rome over various areas, particularly Syria, and had almost as much power as her brother. Although she was married three times to three different kings, the marriages did not last long and she spent most of her life in Agrippa's court. There were constant rumors of an incestuous relationship between the two. Indeed, Agrippa never married.

Festus outranked them. His deference to them stems from their lifelong involvement in Roman politics. Agrippa would one day become a "praetor," one of the most powerful political titles in Rome. Bernice would become the mistress of Emperor Titus (and almost managed to become the Empress). Historians have called her "the Little Cleopatra."

Agrippa and Bernice have no authority over Paul at this point, because the law requires that he be sent to Rome. Due to their high status in Rome, however, Festus diplomatically allows them to interfere. So Paul will have to undergo another meaningless trial.

Day 118 - Paul Before Agrippa and Bernice (1)

Acts 25:23-27

The next day Agrippa and Bernice came with great pomp and entered the auditorium, along with the commanders and leading men of the city. And Festus ordered that Paul be brought in.

Then Festus said, "King Agrippa and all who are present with us, you see this man. The whole Jewish community has petitioned me about him, both here and in Jerusalem, crying out that he ought not to live any longer. But I found he had done nothing worthy of death, and since he has now appealed to the Emperor, I decided to send him.

I have nothing definite to write to our sovereign about him. Therefore I have brought him before all of you, and especially before you, King Agrippa, so that after this inquiry I may have something to write. For it seems unreasonable to me to send on a prisoner without specifying the charges against him."

Commentary

Today, Festus shows his political and diplomatic skills. As the Emperor's representative, he cannot delegate his authority over a Roman citizen, not even to King Agrippa; for Festus represents Rome, while Agrippa's formal position is a client king, subordinate to Rome.

On the other hand, Agrippa and his sister Bernice have enormous personal influence in Rome. They are allies of the emperor and are not to be trifled with.

Festus thus cannot allow them to sit in judgment of a Roman citizen, but neither can he refuse to let them examine Paul. He solves his predicament by casting the hearing as an examination or investigation, the purpose of which is to develop a document that he can send to Rome explaining why Paul is on trial. In other words, he asks for Agrippa's help in clarifying the charges against Paul. This way, he cleverly manages not to offend Agrippa's pride, and at the same time, does not undermine his own authority.

He also makes sure that Agrippa knows Paul has appealed to Rome; this warns Agrippa not to make a judgment, which would become an embarrassment when Festus refuses to carry it out, as he would have to do.

Acts 26 – Paul's Defense to Agrippa

Day 119 - Paul Before Agrippa and Bernice (2)

Acts 26:1-11

Agrippa said to Paul, "You have permission to speak for yourself."

Then Paul stretched out his hand and began his defense: "King Agrippa, I consider myself fortunate to stand before you today to defend myself against all the accusations of the Jews, especially since you are acquainted with all the Jewish customs and controversies. I beg you, therefore, to listen to me patiently.

Surely all the Jews know how I have lived from my earliest childhood among my own people, and also in Jerusalem. They have known me for a long time and can testify, if they are willing, that I lived as a Pharisee, adhering to the strictest sect of our religion.

And now I stand on trial because of my hope in the promise that God made to our fathers, the promise our twelve tribes are hoping to see fulfilled as they earnestly serve God day and night. It is because of this hope, O king, that I am accused by the Jews. Why would any of you consider it incredible that God raises the dead?

So then, I too was convinced that I ought to do all I could to oppose the name of Jesus of Nazareth. And that is what I did in Jerusalem. With authority from the chief priests I put many of the saints in prison, and when they were condemned to death, I cast my vote against them. I frequently had them punished in the synagogues, and I tried to make them blaspheme. In my raging fury against them, I even went to foreign cities to persecute them."

Commentary

Paul did not usually speak to the intellect of his listeners. Nor did he recite a third-person history of Christ and the Holy Spirit. Rather, he talked about himself. He was the great proponent of the new Christian method of preaching: Witnessing to the power of a Christ by the power of a Holy Spirit that lived within him, although he, himself, had not known Jesus in the flesh.

This intimate sharing of one's personal life was a new and convincing type of religious argument. Other parts of the world had dabbled in monotheism, but their concept of God was in their mind. Paul's God was in his heart and spirit. He preached not a god who lived in a statue or even (in the case of the Jews) inside a special place in a temple; he preached the truly universal God, whose Spirit lived in him and colored every moment of his time and every action of his life.

Paul's account here differs, not in facts, but in how he frames his conversion and mission. He more clearly depicts himself as a Jewish prophet. Rather than a revolutionary, he casts himself as a prophet of the evolution of God's promise to Israel. He then shows that he, himself, had once been in Agrippa's position—a Jew who did not accept Jesus and, in fact, persecuted those who did.

We will see tomorrow if his argument can affect the haughty Agrippa.

Day 120 - Paul Before Agrippa and Bernice (3)

Acts 26:12-23

"In this pursuit I was on my way to Damascus with the authority and commission of the chief priests. About noon, O king, as I was on the road, I saw a light from heaven, brighter than the sun, shining around me and my companions. We all fell to the ground, and I heard a voice say to me in Hebrew, 'Saul, Saul, why do you persecute Me? It is hard for you to kick against the goads.'

'Who are You, Lord?' I asked.

'I am Jesus, whom you are persecuting,' the Lord replied. 'But get up and stand on your feet. For I have appeared to you to appoint you as a servant and as a witness of what you have seen from Me and what I will show you. I will rescue you from your own people and from the Gentiles. I am sending you to them to open their eyes, so that they may turn from darkness to light and from the power of Satan to God, that they may receive forgiveness of sins and an inheritance among those sanctified by faith in Me.'

So then, King Agrippa, I was not disobedient to the heavenly vision. First to those in Damascus and Jerusalem, then to everyone in the region of Judea, and then to the Gentiles, I declared that they should repent and turn to God, performing deeds worthy of their repentance. For this reason the Jews seized me in the temple courts and tried to kill me.

But I have had God's help to this day, and I stand here to testify to small and great alike. I am saying nothing beyond what the prophets and Moses said would happen: that the Christ would suffer, and as the first to rise from the dead, would proclaim light to our people and to the Gentiles."

Commentary

The conversion of Saint Paul is told three times in the Bible. The first time, in Acts 9, is the basic chronological story, told in the third person, simply to acquaint the reader with the facts.

The second and third tellings are first-hand accounts, told by Paul himself in defense of accusations against him. The second, in Acts 22, was given to the mob in Jerusalem who were rioting against him.

This third account is part of Paul's defense before Agrippa and his sister Bernice. You can see slight differences in this version from the others.

First, Paul emphasizes his obedience in this telling. He was speaking to convince a king and a governor, who would have valued obedience from the Jewish population above all else. The one thing certain to get Paul executed would be if he appeared to be a revolutionary; thus, rather than emphasize his differences with the Jewish high priests, he emphasizes his obedience to God. He also points out that his teaching is not new, but rather something promised by Moses and other prophets — religious authorities with whom the Jewish Agrippa would be comfortable.

Paul also emphasizes how public his subsequent teachings have been. The cult of Christianity had become fairly large and widespread by this time. Paul wants to assure both king and governor that it is not a secret society, by letting them know that the entire doctrine has always been open (and, thus, not at all concerned with politics). Again, this would quiet any fears they might have of political revolt. Revolutionary groups would often begin with a benign public appearance but would hold secret meetings where the more dangerous aspects of doctrine were given only to members.

Day 121 - Paul Before Agrippa and Bernice (4)

Acts 26:24-32

At this stage of Paul's defense, Festus exclaimed in a loud voice, "You are insane, Paul! Your great learning is driving you to madness!"

But Paul answered, "I am not insane, most excellent Festus; I am speaking words of truth and sobriety. For the king knows about these matters, and I can speak freely to him. I am confident that none of this has escaped his notice, because it was not done in a corner. King Agrippa, do you believe the prophets? I know you do."

Then Agrippa said to Paul, "Can you persuade me in such a short time to become a Christian?"

"Short time or long," Paul replied, "I wish to God that not only you but all who hear me this day may become what I am, except for these chains."

Then the king and the governor rose, along with Bernice and those seated with them. On their way out, they said to one another, "This man has done nothing worthy of death or imprisonment."

And Agrippa said to Festus, "This man could have been released if he had not appealed to Caesar."

Commentary

Porcius Festus, the Roman governor, is by no means the first person to tell Paul he is crazy. In fact, one might imagine that innumerable persons who had heard him speak of raising people from the dead, flashes of light, and voices from God—not to mention his account of

Jesus—would simply think he was schizophrenic. Imagine him speaking in a park today. Passers-by would dismiss him as a raving lunatic.

Jews, however, often take what he says more seriously, as he speaks on subjects many of them believe in deeply: the law and the prophets. Agrippa, a Jew himself, says he is almost persuaded, but it is hard to know what he meant. It might simply be the kind of lie many politicians tell easily and almost automatically. Or he might be genuinely moved, to the point that only his importance and high station prevent him from making the step to salvation.

The three notables agree that Paul has done nothing wrong. But it is easy for them to say that Paul "might have been set free" if he had not appealed to Rome. Empty words are easily spoken. They have no real power to convict or exculpate Paul — he must be sent to Rome.

And, one must notice, it is not in Paul's best interest to be "set free" anyway. A determined cabal of Jews have sworn to murder him. A return to Jerusalem would mean certain death; and even if he had been released in Caesarea, his chances of survival were slim.

Acts 27 – Paul Sails for Rome

Day 122 - Paul's Fourth Journey - Paul Sets Sail for Rome

Acts 27:1-7

When it was decided that we would sail for Italy, Paul and some other prisoners were handed over to a centurion named Julius, who belonged to the Imperial Regiment. We boarded an Adramyttian ship about to sail for ports along the coast of Asia, and we put out to sea. Aristarchus, a Macedonian from Thessalonica, was with us.

The next day we landed at Sidon, and Julius treated Paul with consideration, allowing him to visit his friends and receive their care. After putting out from there, we sailed to the lee of Cyprus because the winds were against us. And when we had sailed across the open sea off the coast of Cilicia and Pamphylia, we came to Myra in Lycia. There the centurion found an Alexandrian ship sailing for Italy and put us on board.

After sailing slowly for many days, we arrived off Cnidus. When the wind impeded us, we sailed to the lee of Crete, opposite Salmone. After we had moved along the coast with difficulty, we came to a place called Fair Havens, near the town of Lasea.

Commentary

Although we call this "Paul's Fourth Journey," it differs from the first three in fundamental ways. It is not entirely voluntary; Paul's only choices are a trial in Jerusalem or a trial in Rome. He is still in custody, a prisoner. (Luckily, Paul seems to be getting lenient treatment from his guard, more like a passenger than a prisoner in chains.) He does not have control over his itinerary; he could not choose, for example, to stay in Ephesus for three years. And the primary purpose of the voyage is not to spread Christ's word. He is, rather, being transferred to a different trial venue by the Roman authorities.

But there are also similarities to his earlier voyages. It will be a long and treacherous trip to a place he has never been; and he will preach and spread Christ's word to new lands, to people who would not have heard him otherwise.

Day 123 - Paul's Warning is Ignored

Acts 27:9-12

By now much time had passed, and the voyage had already become dangerous because it was after the Fast. So Paul advised them, "Men, I can see that our voyage will be filled with disaster and great loss, not only to ship and cargo, but to our own lives as well."

But contrary to Paul's advice, the centurion was persuaded by the pilot and by the owner of the ship. Since the harbor was unsuitable to winter in, the majority decided to sail on, hoping that somehow they could reach Phoenix to winter there. Phoenix was a harbor in Crete facing both southwest and northwest.

Commentary

Paul's ship is most likely an imperial grain ship, which brought grain from the eastern Mediterranean to Rome. The season for these ships was spring and summer; in winter the winds blow the wrong way and create dangerous storms. So the owners are probably trying to eke out extra profit by making another, more dangerous run in early autumn; the pilot and crew thus have a financial interest in getting to Italy promptly, which has led them to their predicament.

The end of the "Fast" — the Jewish Day of Atonement — would have been in early October, so this ship is departing unusually late in the year: a time of shorter days, longer nights, increasing rain and snow, and heavy westerly winds pushing against them.

By this point, they are already in trouble. Although they have scratched and clawed their way to Fair Havens, they have a difficult decision: winter in an unsafe harbor, or risk the adverse conditions to reach a safer harbor at the western tip of Crete. They run for it.

The broad metaphor of the Roman centurion trusting in the pilot and owner — the servants of mammon — rather than in Paul, the servant of God, is difficult to miss. They are going to learn the lesson in Proverbs 3:5-6 the hard way: "Trust in the Lord with all your heart, and do not lean on your own understanding. In all your ways acknowledge him, and he will make straight your paths."

Day 124 - Storm at Sea (1)

Acts 27:13-20

When a gentle south wind began to blow, they thought they had their opportunity. So they weighed anchor and sailed along, hugging the coast of Crete. But it was not long before a cyclone called the Northeaster swept down across the island. Unable to head into the wind, the ship was caught up. So we gave way and let ourselves be driven along.

Passing to the lee of a small island called Cauda, we barely managed to secure the lifeboat. After hoisting it up, the crew used ropes to undergird the ship. And fearing that they would run aground on the sandbars of Syrtis, they lowered the sea anchor and were driven along.

We were tossed so violently that the next day the men began to jettison the cargo. On the third day, they threw the ship's tackle overboard with their own hands. When neither sun nor stars appeared for many days and the great storm continued to batter us, we abandoned all hope of being saved.

Commentary

When a mild wind begins to blow from the south, the captain of Paul's ship gambles — and loses. Before they can make safe harbor at the eastern tip of Crete, a winter storm overpowers them and blows them southwest. They manage to haul in the ship's boat and desperately try to bolster the hull of the ship, to keep the ship from simply being blown apart, but things get worse and worse. So they throw everything that's not nailed down overboard.

But the storm just keeps coming. They finally abandon hope and await their doom.

Around 1575, a Spanish priest (St. John of the Cross) wrote a poem called "The Dark Night of the Soul," to memorialize his wrongful imprisonment. This wonderful term perfectly describes the situation of Paul and his band of travelers. They are literally facing a dark night of utter despair. They are about to die in the middle of the vast ocean; they have not seen the sun for days. As we will see, they are so close to death that they have stopped eating.

But we remember that they reached this sorry state by ignoring God's instructions, given through Paul. So the physical darkness parallels their spiritual darkness; they have refused to follow God's instructions because they cannot see God in their souls, just as they cannot see the sun. No light comes to them from the heavens. And without light, they will die.

We see similar crises of faith a number of times in the Old Testament. It is the central theme of *Job* and several psalms, particularly *Psalm 22*.

Day 125 - Storm at Sea (2)

Acts 27:21-26

After the men had gone a long time without food, Paul stood up among them and said, "Men, you should have followed my advice not to sail from Crete. Then you would have averted this disaster and loss. But now I urge you to keep up your courage, because you will not experience any loss of life, but only of the ship.

For just last night an angel of the God to whom I belong and whom I serve stood beside me and said, 'Do not be afraid, Paul; you must stand before Caesar. And look, God has granted you the lives of all who sail with you.'

So take courage, men, for I believe God that it will happen just as He told me. However, we must run aground on some island."

Commentary

The grain ship from Lycia, on which Paul is being transported to Rome for trial, is in dire trouble. They are lost in a storm south of Crete and have jettisoned the cargo and ship's tackle. They have practically given themselves up for dead.

Isn't it just like Paul to stand up and say, "I told you so"? Which he does with alacrity. Admittedly, he has good reason, since he needs to gain their confidence so that they will follow him.

If Paul shows a tiny bit of pride from time to time, his best qualities shine forth here. He has the heart of a lion and utter faith, and with it, the ability to lead men into salvation no matter how bad things look. Into their world of despair, he brings a lamp of hope that will not flicker or die. Notice, especially how Paul describes his relationship with God: "the God to whom I belong."

The story of Paul's shipwreck is steeped in metaphor. The unpredictable and dangerous sea is an allegorical world of men, and the ship is as lost as the nations and persons who do not know God. The ship (our human vessel) will be lost, yet the men (our eternal soul) will live. But the ship "must run aground" before Paul is brought before Caesar.

Paul brings them the hope of life at their darkest hour; he will lead the crew to the salvation of land with the total confidence he has shown time and time again, in bringing the people of Greece and Anatolia to the salvation of Christ.

Remember the promise that Paul must "stand before Caesar." We know he will not die before God's promise is fulfilled.

Day 126 - Storm at Sea (3)

Acts 27:27-38

On the fourteenth night we were still being driven across the Adriatic Sea. About midnight the sailors sensed they were approaching land. They took soundings and found that the water was twenty fathoms deep. Going a little farther, they took another set of soundings that read fifteen fathoms. Fearing that we would run aground on the rocks, they dropped four anchors from the stern and prayed for daybreak.

Meanwhile, the sailors attempted to escape from the ship. Pretending to lower anchors from the bow, they let the lifeboat down into the sea. But Paul said to the centurion and the soldiers, "Unless these men remain with the ship, you cannot be saved." So the soldiers cut the ropes to the lifeboat and set it adrift.

Right up to daybreak, Paul kept urging them all to eat: "Today is your fourteenth day in constant suspense, without taking any food. So for your own preservation, I urge you to eat something, because not a single hair of your head will be lost."

After he had said this, Paul took bread and gave thanks to God in front of them all. Then he broke it and began to eat. They were all encouraged and took some food themselves. In all, there were 276 of us on board. After the men had eaten their fill, they lightened the ship by throwing the grain into the sea.

Commentary

Have you noticed that this "lost at sea" story is being told in the first person? The narrator (most likely Luke the Evangelist) was actually on the ship and lived through the ordeal, which heightens the drama of the story-telling. The Bible is full of great stories, and this one — the last real "story" in the Bible and also the most recent one — is as exciting as any of them. It could have been told by Herman Melville or Jack London.

The ship is now firmly in Paul's control. There are "no atheists in the foxholes," and the soldiers have turned to their only source of faith and hope—Paul, who is at his best in times of crisis.

The Christian allegory of the story also continues into this passage. The entire ship's company have a metaphorical Last Supper and then, in an act of complete faith, jettison their food stores. Paul has promised them life, just as Christ promised eternal life, and they believe. And their belief will save them.

Day 127 - Paul is Shipwrecked

Acts 27:39-44

When daylight came, they did not recognize the land, but they sighted a bay with a sandy beach, where they decided to run the ship aground if they could. Cutting away the anchors, they left them in the sea as they loosened the ropes that held the rudders. Then they hoisted the foresail to the wind and made for the beach. But the ship struck a sandbar and ran aground. The bow stuck fast and would not move, and the stern was being broken up by the pounding of the waves.

The soldiers planned to kill the prisoners so none of them could swim to freedom. But the centurion, wanting to spare Paul's life, thwarted their plan. He commanded those who could swim to jump overboard first and get to land. The rest were to follow on planks and various parts of the ship. In this way everyone was brought safely to land.

Commentary

Just when the ships' company believes they are safe, having spied a nice cozy beach, one last disaster strikes: they run aground on a reef or sandbar. But Paul, with the help of the centurion, makes sure everybody gets ashore in one piece.

It is difficult to recreate in our minds exactly how dangerous and terrifying their ordeal of a storm at sea was. The Romans were geniuses at engineering; for example, London's streets, sewers, public hygiene, and water supply declined precipitously after Rome abandoned Londinium and did not recover the same level until late in Victoria's reign. But the Romans never applied this genius to shipbuilding.

Roman ships differed only incrementally from those developed by the Phoenicians. These were shallow-draft, square-rigged ships without adequate jibs, and could not handle adverse winds or heavy seas. Paul's grain ship would have been perhaps 80 feet long.

These ships were primarily built to sail along the coastline, staying in sight of land; however, the Romans did send them across the Mediterranean during the calm spring and summer, taking advantage of prevailing winds, especially to haul grain and other goods from north Africa to Italy. They simply did not have the structural strength or design to hold together and stay upright and afloat during a heavy storm. Navigation was utterly primitive.

It is a literal miracle that Paul and the ship's company were not killed. They were blown in a tiny ship by a gale, having neither power nor any idea where they were, five hundred miles across the Mediterranean Sea.

Acts 28 – Paul in Malta and Rome

Day 128 - Malta

Acts 28:1-6

Once we were safely ashore, we learned that the island was called Malta. The islanders showed us extraordinary kindness. They kindled a fire and welcomed all of us because it was raining and cold.

Paul gathered a bundle of sticks, and as he laid them on the fire, a viper, driven out by the heat, fastened itself to his hand. When the islanders saw the creature hanging from his hand, they said to one another, "Surely this man is a murderer. Although he was saved from the sea, Justice has not allowed him to live."

But Paul shook the creature off into the fire and suffered no ill effects. The islanders were expecting him to swell up or suddenly drop dead. But after waiting a long time and seeing nothing unusual happen to him, they changed their minds and said he was a god.

Commentary

By a miracle—literally the hand of God—Paul and his shipmates have stumbled onto Malta. The storm blew them almost 500 miles from Crete onto a tiny speck. Whether Paul's surviving the snakebite was a miracle, however, is open to debate.

One of the most troublesome passages in the Bible, for most Christians, is Mark 16:18, where the resurrected Christ appears to the Apostles and tells them that they will be able to take up serpents and drink poison without being hurt. While very few people believe that this promise applies to later Christians, it might well have applied to Paul.

(*Note*: Mark 16:9-20 does not appear in all Bibles. The issue of its authenticity is the subject of enormous scholarship and debate. I think the better case is made to include it, but there is a reasonable argument that it is not original.)

It is entirely possible that Paul's recovery was not miraculous at all. Many bites from venomous snakes are "dry bites" — that is, the snake will not inject venom; and very possibly, the snake in this case simply wasn't venomous. There are no snakes on Malta today that can kill a human. In fact, the passage itself does not claim that the snake was dangerous, although the witnesses believed it was.

To further complicate matters, the ecosystem of Malta has changed greatly in the past 2,000 years. (North Africa was so lush 2,000 years ago that it was called the "breadbasket of Rome"!) Today, it would be almost impossible to gather enough wood on Malta to make a fire, as the island is almost devoid of trees, whereas it was heavily forested when Paul landed there. So, we don't know — Malta may well have had deadly snakes in the past. And one would think that the native inhabitants, who feared for Paul's life, would know whether a particular snake was venomous.

So, miracle or luck? It is impossible to know. (One might even say that they are practically the same thing, in God's eye. Many Christians do not believe that "luck" exists.) What is striking about the story, however, is the symbolism. The serpent has represented Satan since *Genesis*; even in non-Judeo/Christian cultures, snakes are often considered the embodiment of evil. Not only is Paul resistant to the evil, but also, he casts the serpent into the fire, the symbol of hell.

The story makes a fitting conclusion to the allegory of Paul's voyage: Having survived the very real dangers of being lost at sea during a storm, in a small wooden ship, Paul finalizes the tale by destroying the serpent to illustrate Christ's final victory over Satan.

Day 129 - Paul on Malta

Acts 28:7-10

Nearby stood an estate belonging to Publius, the chief official of the island. He welcomed us and entertained us hospitably for three days. The father of Publius was sick in bed, suffering from fever and dysentery. Paul went in to see him, and after praying and placing his hands on him, he healed the man. After this had happened, the rest of the sick on the island came and were cured as well.

The islanders honored us in many ways and supplied our needs when we were ready to sail.

Commentary

Malta was a Roman colony. It is an odd island, half-European and half-north-African in language and culture, lying in a critical position between Sicily and the North African coast.

As we mentioned yesterday, the climate and ecology of the Mediterranean were vastly different 2,000 years ago. Malta and Roman "Africa" — which included Carthage (Libya), Tunisia, and part of Algeria — did not lie in an impoverished semi-arid region. The area was green and fertile, ideal for growing grain. It was the breadbasket of southern Europe and fueled first the growth of Greece (e.g. Athens) and, later, Rome.

Malta was thus significant, being the only island lying astride the principal trade route for Rome's food. And Paul sensibly does his best to make friends with its Roman governor, Publius.

There is no account of Paul preaching. He was under arrest, and although he was not kept in chains or jail, no doubt his freedom was curtailed. But we might infer at least some evangelizing, for Paul is performing miracles left and right, healing the dying and shaking off a snake. How could he not have taken the opportunity to tell the people there about Christ?

Day 130 - Paul Arrives at Rome

Acts 28:11-16

After three months we set sail in an Alexandrian ship that had wintered in the island. It had the Twin Brothers as a figurehead. Putting in at Syracuse, we stayed there three days. From there we weighed anchor and came to Rhegium. After one day, a south wind came up, and on the second day we arrived at Puteoli. There we found some brothers who invited us to spend the week with them. And so we came to Rome.

The brothers there had heard about us and traveled as far as the Forum of Appius and the Three Taverns to meet us. When Paul saw them, he was encouraged and gave thanks to God.

When we arrived in Rome, Paul was permitted to stay by himself, with a soldier to guard him.

Commentary

Paul and his company have found an Egyptian grain ship which tried to do what they themselves had tried — to make one last run before the winter storms started — only were quite a bit luckier (or smarter) to lay over in Malta. The ship's name, the "twin gods" or "Twin Brothers," refers to Castor and Pollux, minor Greek gods thought by the Greeks to protect sailors.

In the first century, the port of Puteoli, situated on the Bay of Naples ten miles from the City of Naples, was the regular terminus for Egyptian trade. It was the second most important port in all of Italy (after Ostia, which was the port of the City of Rome) since it received so much of the grain Rome needed to survive. The famous Appian Way ran by Puteoli straight to Rome, 170 miles distant. It is a tribute to Roman engineering that cars can still drive upon it today!

Once they arrive, Paul is put under house arrest. One can only imagine that the commander of the guard might have spoken well of him to the authorities when they arrived in Rome. But it is a most fortunate circumstance, as it will allow Paul to continue his mission in the world's greatest city.

In fact, in his *Epistle to the Romans*, Paul stated that it had been his intention (for many years) to go next to Rome and help the church there. Rome's Christian community had grown without the needed guidance of one of the apostles. So perhaps, during his trials in Judea, he intended to appeal to Rome all along, that he might get free transport to a place he wanted to visit.

Application Question: "Unintended Consequences"

Paul wanted to go to Rome, but he got there in a roundabout manner, to say the least. God surely intended that Paul end up in Rome, all along.

Have you had instances in your life where you tried to do something, but God seemed to have different ideas, and you ended up where you were "supposed to be" rather than where you intended to be?

And if you are wondering where you are headed right now, I hope you will take comfort from Paul's story; for God will eventually send us where He wants us.

Day 131 - Paul in Rome (1)

Acts 28:17-22

After three days, he called together the leaders of the Jews. When they had gathered, he said to them, "Brothers, although I have done nothing against our people or the customs of our fathers, I was taken prisoner in Jerusalem and handed over to the Romans. They examined me and wanted to release me, because there was no basis for a death sentence against me.

But when the Jews objected, I was compelled to appeal to Caesar, even though I have no charge to bring against my nation. So for this reason I have called to see you and speak with you. It is because of the hope of Israel that I am bound with this chain."

The leaders replied, "We have not received any letters about you from Judea, nor have any of the brothers from there reported or even mentioned anything bad about you. But we consider your views worth hearing, because we know that people everywhere are speaking against this sect."

Commentary

Only three days pass in Rome before Paul calls the local Jewish leaders to visit him, to prevent them from fomenting hostility towards him. He wants to make sure they hear his side of the story, lest the authorities in Jerusalem enlist them to persecute him. Remember, a number of Jews in Jerusalem had sworn that they would not eat until they had murdered Paul — their dislike of him was that strong. (I imagine they were getting pretty hungry by now.)

Luckily, he speaks to them in time. None of them have gotten letters or messengers poisoning their minds against Paul. Christianity, however, has gotten a bad name among them; undoubtedly, angry Jews from Macedonia and possibly Anatolia have visited Rome. Remember, for example, in Acts 17, where a group of Jews from Thessalonica had followed Paul to other cities, trying to suppress and possibly kill him.

And so, wanting more information about "this sect," they ask Paul for his view — which is actually rather funny, because Paul is going to tell them about Christ, whether they want to hear it or not.

Day 132 - Paul in Rome (2)

Acts 28:23-28

So they set a day to meet with Paul, and many people came to the place he was staying. He expounded to them from morning to evening, testifying about the kingdom of God and persuading them about Jesus from the Law of Moses and the Prophets.

Some of them were convinced by what he said, but others refused to believe. They disagreed among themselves and began to leave after Paul had made this final statement: "The Holy Spirit was right when He spoke to your fathers through Isaiah the prophet:

'Go to this people and say,
"You will be ever hearing but never understanding;
you will be ever seeing but never perceiving."
For this people's heart has grown callous;
they hardly hear with their ears,

and they have closed their eyes.
Otherwise they might see with their eyes,
hear with their ears,
understand with their hearts,
and turn, and I would heal them.' *[Isaiah 6:9-10]*

Be advised, therefore, that God's salvation has been sent to the Gentiles, and they will listen!"

Commentary

After Paul's initial meeting with the Jewish leaders, they return; and not just them, but a number of other people. Paul begins to preach "from morning to evening" and succeeds in making some converts—but only in his house. The Romans are lenient with Paul, but his house arrest apparently precludes preaching from public places.

He converts some of the Jews; those who will not be convinced, he criticizes with a famous passage from Isaiah (Isaiah 6:9-10). The reason for their leaving is not stated. Perhaps they have heard all they can absorb in one sitting and are just ready to go and debate Paul's teachings among themselves. They would certainly have needed to consider Paul's statement, "this salvation of God has been sent to the Gentiles."

The Old Testament supports Paul's words, however, specifically that the covenant between God and the Hebrews was created to benefit all the people of Earth. *E.g.*, Genesis 18:18, "Abraham will surely become a great and mighty nation, and in him all the nations of the earth will be blessed." According to *Isaiah*, the Messiah would be "a light for the Gentiles, that my salvation may reach to the end of the earth." (Isaiah 49:6)

But many Jews (like many Christians today) ignored whatever parts of the Bible did not suit their preconceptions or convenience. Paul's preaching to Gentiles and the acceptance of Gentiles as equals in the Christian churches offended many Jews, who had come to see themselves as eternally special, the only people who could live in God's grace.

Even for those who accepted Paul's teaching, his mention of salvation for the Gentiles would have come as a shock. Both groups of Jews

— those who were convinced by him and those who opposed him — left to argue and discuss all they had heard.

CONCLUSION

Day 133 - Paul in Rome (3)

Acts 28:30-31

Paul stayed there two full years in his own rented house, welcoming all who came to visit him. Boldly and freely he proclaimed the kingdom of God and taught about the Lord Jesus Christ.

Commentary

And so ends the *Book of Acts*, with Paul awaiting trial. There was no contemporary account written of what befell him thereafter. Many histories written in the next century, however, inform us that Paul was tried and released. This would make sense. Paul was not accused of anything that would offend Rome, and his enemies did not have any political pull there. We also know that people who did have political pull in Rome—Herod Agrippa II, his sister Bernice, and Festus Porcius—seemed favorably disposed towards him.

According to these non-Biblical accounts, after his acquittal Paul took a fifth missionary journey, traveling as far as Spain. The accounts are generally credible.

Particularly well-attested is a letter written by Clement of Rome in 95 A.D. (Clement was a close successor of Peter as a bishop of Rome and is listed by the Catholic Church as the fourth pope. He took office just 25 years after Peter's execution.) Clement wrote that Paul "reached the farthest limits of the West," which would include Spain, without doubt. Other second-century fragmentary documents mention Paul in Spain.

Spain was an enormously important part of the Roman Empire; travel to Spain by either ship or land was comparatively easy and safe, for that time. There were also early Christian churches in Spain. James (the Greater), the patron saint of Spain, is believed to have traveled to

Spain in a very early mission, before he was martyred in Jerusalem (Acts 12:1-2). Philip the Apostle was also credited with a mission to Spain.

In fact, numerous scholars believe that Paul's mission in Rome was part of a plan. While establishing a solid and active church in Rome was an end in itself, it also created an anchor to support the Spanish (and French) churches, which were a long way from Antioch and Ephesus!

Years later, when he had visited Spain, Paul was arrested again, after Nero began his erratic persecution against Christians; he returned to Rome for trial and was beheaded there.

I hope you have found this work useful in your path to spiritual growth. I appreciate criticism and comments, so feel free to email me at https://form.jotform.com/240465082287156.

And by all means, come pray and study with us at https://dailyprayer.us or https://dailydevotion.org. We have new devotions every day, 365 days a year!

MAP

See next page.

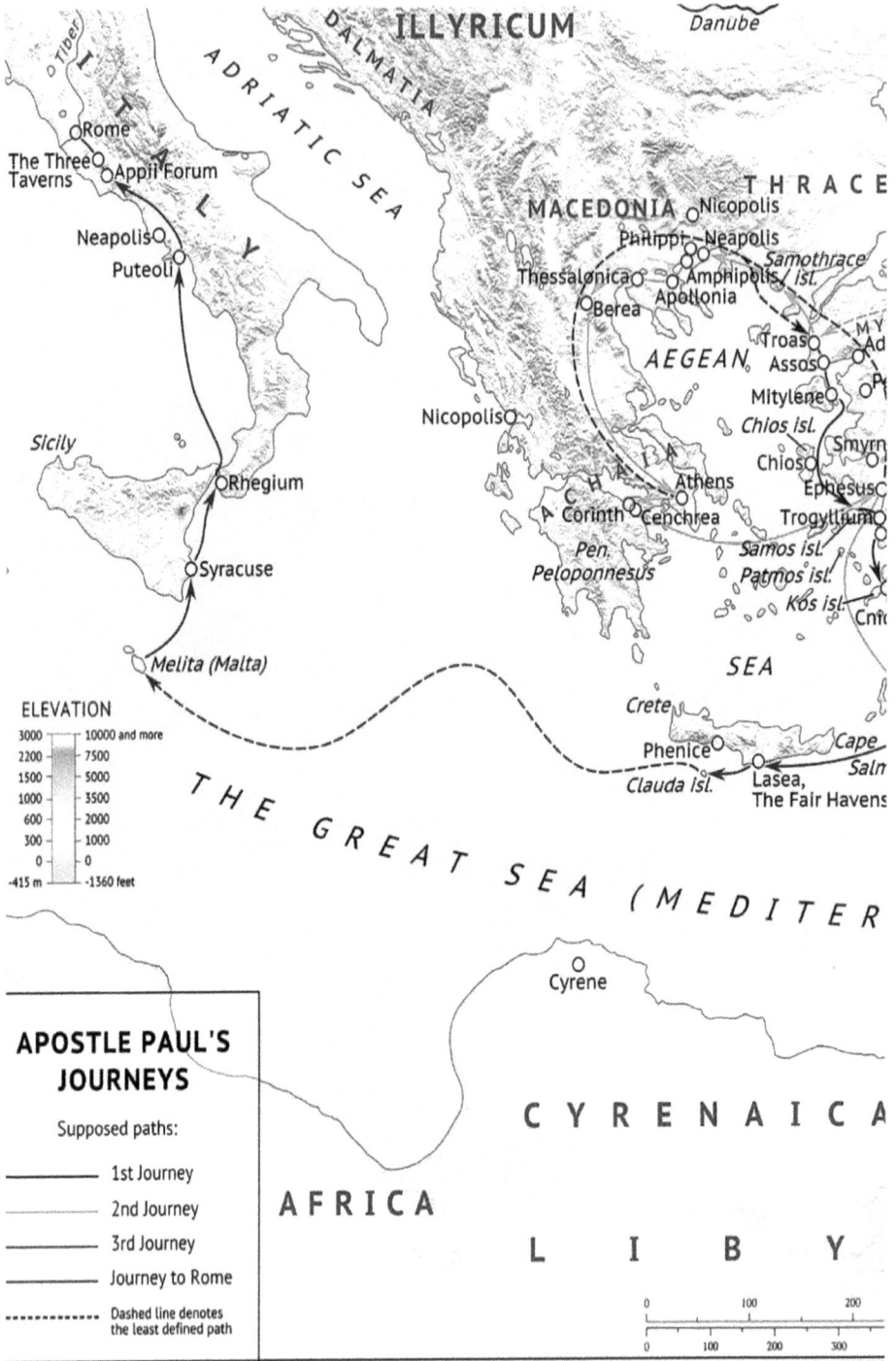

ELEVATION

3000	10000 and more
2200	7500
1500	5000
1000	3500
600	2000
300	1000
0	0
-415 m	-1360 feet

APOSTLE PAUL'S JOURNEYS

Supposed paths:

———— 1st Journey

———— 2nd Journey

———— 3rd Journey

———— Journey to Rome

--------- Dashed line denotes the least defined path

PONTUS EUXINUS
(BLACK SEA)

Sinope

THRACE

BITHYNIA

PONTUS

Ancyra

Halys

CAPPADOCIA

MYSIA

Troas
Assos
Adramyttium
Pergamos
Mitylene
Thyatira
Chios isl.
Sardis
Smyrna
Philadelphia
Chios
Ephesus
Hierapolis
Trogyllium
Laodicea Colosse
Samos isl.
Miletus
Patmos isl.
Kos
Kos isl.
Cnidus
Rhodes
Rhodes isl.

ASIA

PHRYGIA

LYCAONIA

Antioch
Iconium
Lystra
Derbe

PISIDIA

PAMPHYLIA

Attalia
Perga
LYCIA
Patara
Myra

Samothrace isl.

Haran

Euphrates

Tarsus

CILICIA

Seleucia
Antioch

SYRIA

Salamis

Paphos

Cyprus

Cape
Salmone

Lasea,
The Fair Havens

EA

Sidon

Damascus

Tyre
Ptolemais

PHOENICIA

(MEDITERRANEAN SEA)

Caesarea
Joppa
Azotus
Gaza

Nazareth
Samaria
Jordan
Jerusalem
Bethlehem
DEAD (SALT) SEA

Alexandria

AICA

Y A

EGYPT

Nile

Memphis

Sinai
Peninsula

RED SEA

ARABIA

100   200   300 ml
200   300   400   500 km

Free for any usage (Public domain)
2020. Map version 1.5
-churchmaps.info

About the Author

Mason Barge (BA Yale University, JD Emory University, MBS Andersonville Theological Seminary) is the Editor-in-Chief of Daily Prayer Ministries, Inc., in Atlanta, Georgia, and is the author of over 1,500 Biblical commentaries. His primary ministry is online, through the website titled "Daily Prayer." This site provides a non-denominational, non-political Daily Devotion every day.

https://dailyprayer.us

or

https://dailydevotion.org

Daily Prayer Ministries also maintains a daily page on Facebook with over 750,000 followers.

https://www.facebook.com/DailyPrayer.us/

Mr. Barge lives in Atlanta, Georgia, and attends Midtown Church.

Acknowledgements

Unless otherwise noted, all Scripture is taken from the *Berean Standard Bible*, with many thanks.

Many thanks to my wonderful editor, Sarah Pringle. God bless you! My deepest thanks to Roger Quillen and Greg Riner for reading through the final draft and making many helpful suggestions and corrections.

Cover painting: *Landscape with Christ and His Disciples on the Road to Emmaus*, by Jan Wildens, ca. 1640.

Cover photo by John Carter.

Maps courtesy of Yuriy Konstantynov (churchmaps.info)

CliffsNotes is the registered trademark of COURSE HERO, INC.

The text of this book is set in EB Garamond. The headings are set in Calibri Light.

www.ingramcontent.com/pod-product-compliance
Lightning Source LLC
Chambersburg PA
CBHW060154070426
42447CB00033B/1335